W9-CGN-574

HAYEK ON HAYEK

F. A. HAYEK

THE COLLECTED WORKS OF

F. A. Hayek

HAYEK ON HAYEK

An Autobiographical Dialogue

F. A. HAYEK

Edited by Stephen Kresge and Leif Wenar

Liberty Fund

INDIANAPOLIS

This book is published by Liberty Fund, Inc., a foundation established to encourage study of the ideal of a society of free and responsible individuals.

The cuneiform inscription that serves as our logo and as the design motif for our endpapers is the earliest-known written appearance of the word "freedom" (*amagi*), or "liberty." It is taken from a clay document written about 2300 B.C. in the Sumerian city-state of Lagash.

Hayek on Hayek is a supplement to The Collected Works of F. A. Hayek, published by The University of Chicago Press.

This Liberty Fund paperback edition of *Hayek on Hayek* is published by arrangement with The University of Chicago Press and Taylor & Francis Books, Ltd., a member of the Taylor & Francis Group.

© 1994 by The Bartley Institute

Excerpts of interviews from the Bartley archive of audiotapes are printed with the permission of Stephen Kresge. Excerpts of interviews conducted by the Oral History Program, University of California, Los Angeles, © Regents of the University of California, have been published by permission. Excerpts of Thomas Hazlett's interview with F. A. Hayek are reprinted, with permission, from *Reason* magazine (July 1992). © 1992 by the Reason Foundation, 3415 S. Sepulveda Blvd., Suite 400, Los Angeles, CA 90034. In the introduction, excerpts of letters from F. A. Hayek to Karl Popper are used with the permission of the estate of F. A. Hayek; excerpts of a letter from Karl Popper to Hayek, quoting Rudolf Carnap, are used with the permission of Sir Karl Popper. Illustrations are from the Bartley archive and are reproduced with the permission of Stephen Kresge.

Frontispiece: Friedrich Hayek © Bettmann/CORBIS
Cover photo: Friedrich August von Hayek © Hulton-Deutsch Collection/CORBIS

All rights reserved
Printed in the United States of America

P   1   2   3   4   5   6   7   8   9   10

Library of Congress Cataloging-in-Publication Data

Hayek, Friedrich A. von (Friedrich August), 1899–1992.
Hayek on Hayek: an autobiographical dialogue/F. A. Hayek; edited by Stephen Kresge and Leif Wenar.—Liberty Fund paperback ed.
p.   cm.
"Hayek on Hayek is a supplement to The Collected Works of F. A. Hayek, published by The University of Chicago Press."
Includes bibliographical references and index.
ISBN 978-0-86597-740-2 (pbk.: alk. paper)
1. Hayek, Friedrich A. von (Friedrich August), 1899–1992—Interviews.   2. Economists—Austria—Biography.   3. Economists—Great Britain—Biography.   4. Economists—Austria—Interviews.   5. Economists—Great Britain—Interviews.   I. Kresge, Stephen.   II. Wenar, Leif.   III. Hayek, Friedrich A. von (Friedrich August), 1899–1992. Works. 1989.   IV. Title.
HB171.H426   2008 Suppl.
330.1—dc22   2008028278

Liberty Fund, Inc.
8335 Allison Pointe Trail, Suite 300
Indianapolis, Indiana 46250-1684

This book is printed on paper that is acid-free and meets the requirements of the American National Standard for Permanence of Paper for Printed Library Materials, Z39.48-1992. ∞

Cover design by Erin Kirk New, Watkinsville, Georgia
Printed and bound by Thomson-Shore, Inc., Dexter, Michigan

THE COLLECTED WORKS OF F. A. HAYEK

Founding Editor: W. W. Bartley III
General Editor: Stephen Kresge
Associate Editor: Peter G. Klein
Assistant Editor: Gene Opton

Published with the support of

The Hoover Institution on War, Revolution and Peace,
Stanford University

Anglo American and De Beers Chairman's Fund, Johannesburg

Cato Institute, Washington, D.C.

The Centre for Independent Studies, Sydney

Chung-Hua Institution for Economic Research, Taipei

Engenharia Comércio e Indústria S/A, Rio de Janeiro

Escuela Superior de Economia y Administración de Empresas
(ESEADE), Buenos Aires

The Heritage Foundation

The Institute for Humane Studies, George Mason University

Instituto Liberal, Rio de Janeiro

Charles G. Koch Charitable Foundation, Wichita

The Carl Menger Institute, Vienna

The Morris Foundation, Little Rock

Verband der Österreichischen Banken und Bankiers, Vienna

The Wincott Foundation, London

The Bartley Institute, Oakland

CONTENTS

See illustrations following page 84

EDITORIAL FOREWORD

The inspiration for *Hayek on Hayek* was F. A. Hayek's own voice. Not so much his speaking voice as a characteristic manner of expression that reveals a cast of mind, his own unique point of view. Would it not be a great benefit to have his own voice as a guide to understand the development of his ideas and to recall the events and experience of the past century to which his ideas responded and out of which they emerged?

Two primary sources are available to produce such a guide. The first source consists of autobiographical notes that Hayek wrote over a period of years beginning in 1945. By way of introduction he observed:

> As my recent election to the British Academy makes it inevitable that at some future date somebody will have to attempt a brief sketch of my life, and as very little will then be known of my life before I came to England, I shall attempt here from time to time, as I feel inclined to it, to set down a few of the more significant features of my background and development. What I shall write is not intended for publication but solely to provide material for whoever will have to undertake the ungrateful task of discovering interesting facts about an externally rather uneventful life. But perhaps some of it will some day be of interest to my children or grandchildren, at any rate if they feel anything like the fascination which the fate of my ancestors has always possessed for me.

Hayek later agreed to the publication of his notes. He had given them to W. W. Bartley III, who had undertaken Hayek's biography. Bartley realized that the notes should be published as they were. When Hayek agreed, he somewhat diffidently suggested that they might be included within a larger biographical work, possibly set off in a different typeface. We have followed that suggestion.

In reading through many interviews with Hayek, we found that he had provided the outline of an intellectual biography. This was, of course, his clear intention in his many talks with Bartley. These and other interviews, particularly those made under the auspices of the Oral History Program at the University of California, Los Angeles, are the second source from which *Hayek on Hayek* has been drawn.

Since there was considerable duplication in the questions Hayek was asked, there was also repetition in his answers. Our task was to select the best of Hayek's own statements on the development of his ideas and the important events of his life. These statements are presented here within the chronological framework provided by Hayek's autobiographical notes. Our wish has been to preserve the authentic voice of Hayek himself, so editing of the material has been kept to a minimum. We have not intruded on the text with any of the usual scholarly apparatus. *Hayek on Hayek* is a conversation, and the ideas for which we read Hayek may be encountered newly alive and accessible.

The volume also includes a lively exchange between Hayek and two University of Chicago professors during a radio broadcast in 1945. The complete transcript is reproduced in part three.

The editors have provided supporting material in the form of selected biographical and bibliographical information included in the name index. An introduction provides a brief account of the historical and intellectual context of Hayek's life work. A list of publications and letters mentioned in the text is given for the benefit of readers who wish to make a more extensive exploration of the material. The interviews excerpted are identified by numbers assigned to the respective interviewers:

Q_1: Oral History Program, Robert Chitester, president, Public Broadcasting of Northwestern Pennsylvania.

Q_2: Oral History Program, Jack High, Department of Economics, UCLA.

Q_3: *Reason* magazine (July 1992), Thomas W. Hazlett.

Q_4: Oral History Program, Earlene Craver, Department of Economics, UCLA.

Q_5: Oral History Program, James Buchanan, Center for the Study of Public Choice, Virginia Polytechnic Institute.

Q_6: W. W. Bartley III audiotape archive, 1984–88.

Q_7: Oral History Program, Axel Leijonhufvud, Department of Economics, UCLA.

Q_8: Oral History Program, Thomas W. Hazlett, Department of Economics, UCLA.

The editors are most grateful to Ms. Gene Opton, assistant editor of The Collected Works of F. A. Hayek, for her scrupulous supervision of every aspect of the production of this work; most of all for her uncanny ability to decipher Hayek's handwriting. We would also like to thank our research assistant, Bryan Caplan; Leslie Graves for her careful reading of the text; and Dr. and Mrs. Laurence Hayek and Miss Christine Hayek for their great kindness and care with so many papers and through so many difficulties. We are grateful to Bruce J. Caldwell, Naomi Moldofsky, Angelo Petroni, and Gerard Radnitzky for additional facts, comments, and criticisms.

Because *Hayek on Hayek* has been produced as a supplement to The Collected Works of F. A. Hayek, we would like to express our gratitude to the sponsors of that project for their continuing support. The editors would particularly like to acknowledge the encouragement and generosity of Walter Morris of the Morris Foundation; John Blundell, now director of the Institute of Economic Affairs; and the Claude R. Lambe Foundation.

Stephen Kresge
Leif Wenar

INTRODUCTION

F. A. Hayek was born Friedrich August von Hayek on May 8, 1899, in Vienna, then the capital of the Austro-Hungarian empire. He died on March 23, 1992, in the city of Freiburg im Breisgau in Germany, a country only recently reunified following the fall of the Berlin Wall and the end of Soviet domination of Eastern Europe.

The collapse of socialism vindicated Hayek's life work. His best-known book, *The Road to Serfdom,* played a critical role in restoring the political and economic ideals that made possible the dismantling of communist regimes. That the Stinger missile, rock music, and blue jeans probably played a more visible part in the process would not have dismayed Hayek. He more than anyone has made us aware that values are transmitted along unpredictable paths.

If the almost one hundred years through which Hayek lived have been dubbed by some the 'American century,' it could also be considered the Austrian century; for it has largely been the intellectual and cultural eruptions from Vienna and Central Europe to which the rest of the world has been forced to respond. The assassination of the Archduke Ferdinand and his wife at Sarajevo on June 28, 1914, set in motion a violent reordering of the course of history.

The war which the Europeans started in 1914, thinking it would last only a matter of months, ended by destroying not just the promise of a generation but the fundamental premises of a civilization. Nationalism and socialism moved into the vacuum left by the self-destruction of empires. Even the basic nature of human beings was called into question. "On or about December 1910, human character changed," wrote Virginia Woolf (in the essay "Mr. Bennett and Mrs. Brown"). But this change in character had failed in its promise.

Hayek joined a field artillery regiment in March 1917, before he had completed his education at the *Gymnasium*. For him the war would last barely more than a year. He returned from the Italian front amidst hunger, disease, and chaos. In November of 1918 he began his studies at the University of Vienna.

The war turned Hayek's interest from the natural sciences to the social sciences, out of the experience of serving in a multinational army. "That's when I saw, more or less, the great empire collapse over the nationalist problem. I served in a battle in which eleven different languages were spoken. It's bound to draw your attention to the problems of political organization," he later recalled (see p. 48).

If the legitimate dominion of empire was now under attack, even less secure was the dominion of the mind. Relativity, quantum mechanics, Freud, Proust, the post-Impressionists, were altering once and for all our notions of physical existence and how we perceive it. "I put down my cup and examine my own mind. It is for it to discover the truth. But how? What an abyss of uncertainty whenever the mind feels that some part of it has strayed beyond its own borders; when it, the seeker, is at once the dark region through which it must go seeking, where all its equipment will avail it nothing. Seek? More than that: create. It is face to face with something which does not so far exist, to which it alone can give reality and substance, which it alone can bring into the light of day." So the narrator begins the long recollection that is Marcel Proust's remembrance of things past.

Years later Hayek completes a similar investigation in *The Sensory Order*, published in 1952. "What we call 'mind' is thus a particular order of a set of events taking place in some organism and in some manner related to but not identical with, the physical order of events in the environment" (*The Sensory Order*, p. 16). "All we know about the world is of the nature of theories, and all 'experience' can do is to change these theories" (*The Sensory Order*, p. 143).

Education

Hayek returned from the war with a knowledge of Italian and a severe infection of malaria. He took up several branches of study at the University of Vienna and fully participated in the social and cultural life of the period, though on alternate nights he would be laid up with fever. When the university closed in the winter of 1919–20 for lack of heating fuel, Hayek went to Zurich, where, in the laboratory of the brain anatomist von Monakow, he had his first encounter with the fibre bundles that make up the human brain, and his first taste of what a 'normal' society could be like, Vienna still being in the throes of inflation and semistarvation. In the summer of 1920 he went to Norway and was finally able to shake the malaria and to acquire enough knowledge of Scandinavian languages to translate a book by Gustav Cassel on inflation (which, owing to the inflation in Austria, was never published).

In these early years at the university, Hayek established the patterns of intellectual investigation that would remain with him his entire life. "In the university, the decisive point was simply that you were not expected to confine yourself to your own subject" (see p. 51). Nor did one confine oneself to the university. Much of the provocative intellectual discussion went on in the coffeehouses. High German was the language of the lectures at the university; a changing vernacular was used in the streets of the city.

Hayek's view of this period is somewhat different from and somewhat more precise than many that have contributed to the mythical characterization of Vienna. He was born into the class which was largely responsible for the maintenance of the Austro-Hungarian empire and which did not survive its collapse. Neither of the higher nobility nor the merchant class, it was a class of civil servants and professionals who were not indifferent to their own advancement but nevertheless maintained standards of conduct and inquiry that linked them to their counterparts throughout Europe.

Hayek's father was a doctor and botanist who had hoped to obtain a full university chair in botany. From him Friedrich August—his mother called him Fritz, an appellation he bore stoically but which he did not care for—gained a sense of the wonder and complexity of biology and psychology and a belief that a university chair was the most desirable of all positions.

Hayek's immediate course of study at the university was driven by practical considerations. Unlike his cousin Ludwig Wittgenstein, he could not count on a family fortune. Thus the first choice of a career which seemed to satisfy his temperament and talents would lead through the study of law and languages to the diplomatic service and perhaps later to an academic or political position. With the collapse of the empire, the *Konsular-akademie* disappeared, and diplomatic ambitions with it.

At the university Hayek still wavered between psychology and economics. But after the war there was no one left to teach psychology, and no possibility of a degree in that field. Law remained as a study which combined economics with preparation for the bar or the civil service. Hayek accomplished his work for a degree in three years rather than the customary four and in 1921 received a doctorate in jurisprudence. He registered for a second degree and early in 1923 received a doctorate in political science (*doctor rerum politicarum*).

The dominant influence on the intellectual life of the period was Ernst Mach. The name Mach is now known to most of us only as a unit of measurement for the speed of supersonic aircraft. Mach's philosophy of science was, to put it crudely, if it can't be measured, it isn't real. Mach's machete (larger and sharper than Ockham's mere razor) cut through the metaphysical thicket that threatened to choke off the development of science.

Mach had been the first professor of the inductive sciences at the University of Vienna. He was followed in the chair which had been created for him by Ludwig Boltzmann, then Adolf Stöhr, then, in 1922, Moritz Schlick. Hayek first heard of Schlick on his visit to Zurich. Schlick was the founder of the *Ernst Mach Verein*—the Vienna circle—which succeeded, by combining an attack on the foundations of logic with a verificationist empiricism, in directing the attention of philosophers to a hapless attempt to distinguish meaningful statements from meaningless ones. Called 'logical positivism,' it led to the sequel of Wittgenstein, whose later work repudiated his early work, and to the antidote of Karl Popper. Though never part of the Vienna circle, Hayek quickly learned of their ideas through a mutual member of Hayek's own group, which called itself the *Geistkreis*.

Hayek's early exposure to the natural sciences left him disposed to accept Mach's contention that all we can know are sensations. Yet the vision of the bundles of brain fibres which he had examined in the winter of 1920 stayed in his mind. He wrote a paper, which ultimately remained unfinished, wherein he tried to trace the progress of sensations (neural impulses) to the brain, where they assume the shape and sense of a perception. By the end of the paper he realized that Mach was wrong. Pure sensations cannot be perceived. Interconnections in the brain must be made; some sort of classification that can relate past experience to present experience must take place. Hayek began to grope his way toward a solution of a problem not previously recognized: How can order create itself? The solution sounded part Kant, part Darwin, even part Proust. It would eventually be pure Hayek.

"What original ideas I have had," Hayek writes (see pp. 134–35), "actually did not come out of an orderly process of reasoning. I have always regarded myself as a living refutation of the contention that all thinking takes place in words or generally in language. I am as certain as I can be that I have often been aware of having the answer to a problem—of 'seeing' it before me—long before I could express it in words. Indeed a sort of visual imagination, of symbolic abstract patterns rather than representational pictures, probably played a bigger role in my mental processes than words." Einstein has said much the same thing.

The perception of patterns is central to all of Hayek's work. It is perhaps a kind of intellectual mountaineering, and mountaineering was in his blood and bone.

"What I had in mind in early years was a purely practical concern, wanting to find my way about, not yet fully aware that to do this I needed a theory. I was in search of a theory, but didn't know yet what a theory really was."

In October 1921 Hayek presented a letter of recommendation from his teacher at the university, Friedrich von Wieser, to Ludwig von Mises, then financial advisor to the Chamber of Commerce (an official body, unlike the American organizations of the same name). Mises found Hayek a position at a temporary agency called the *Abrechnungsamt* [Office of Accounts], of which Mises was one of the directors. The office was engaged in clearing debts that had been blocked by the war. Hayek's knowledge of French and Italian, and later of English, together with his knowledge of law and economics, qualified him for what was a comparatively well-paid job. But the main attraction was the maturing relationship with Ludwig von Mises.

Mises was respected as an economist for his book on the theory of money, published in 1912. Hayek has claimed that during the great inflation which followed the war in both Austria and Germany, and which, more than the war itself, destroyed the class into which Hayek was born, Mises was probably the only person in the German-speaking world who understood what was happening.

In 1922 Mises published his great book on socialism, the work that was to provide the foundation for the case against socialist planning. Mises's argument focused on the role played by freely adjusting prices in a competitive market system. Price adjustments reflect changes in relative scarcities, which signal decision-makers to alter their resource allocations. Without freely adjusting prices, the efficient allocation of resources cannot proceed. Mises's argument ultimately persuaded Hayek to abandon the Fabian tendencies that he had adopted up to that time.

Hayek's first enthusiasm for economics stemmed from his reading of Carl Menger's *Grundsätze der Volkswirtschaftslehre* [*Principles of Economics*], which had been published in 1871 and was the major influence on subsequent generations of Austrian economists. Menger is credited with being among the first (along with Jevons and Walras) to introduce the concept of marginal utility into economics. More significantly, Menger's concept of utility rested on an analysis of the concept of value that was opposed to the theory of value found in classical economics. For Menger, value is not an intrinsic property or essence of any commodity or effort. There is no intrinsic value in land or labor or gold, only the value of the use of such factors; and this value can only be determined in relation to other possible uses. Such relations vary from case to case and individual to individual. Only the individual can know what one is prepared to give up or substitute to obtain the use—that is, the value—of something else.

The requirement that value be rooted in a set of relations—alternatives or substitutions—is fundamental to much of what has been recognized as the 'Austrian' school of economics. In the Austrian theory of capital, the length or complexity of systems of production is altered in response to changes in prices or interest rates. Thus the role of prices and interest rates as guides to investment is crucial.

The subjective, thus indeterminate, nature of value does not sit well with more positivistically inclined economists who are uncomfortable without a fixed basis for measurement. American economists were demonstrating that the limits of what could be measured had not yet been reached. Hayek seized upon the possibility of a research assistantship in New York to travel to the United States. By March 1923, he had saved enough money to pay for a passage to America.

New York and Business Cycles

Looking back at the end of his life, Hayek felt he had been extraordinarily lucky in the way in which one discovery or opportunity led to another. Only his surprising decision to go to New York in 1923 was so out of the ordinary, almost out of character, that he could not really account for it. He even grew a beard for the journey. It is clear that what he brought back from that visit was not altogether what he had expected to find.

He spent most of his time in New York in the public library, and his first shock was reading the American accounts of the Great War. The American newspaper stories of the war were accurate and revealing in a way that the Austrian accounts had not been. The truth about the course of the war had been largely kept from the Austrian people. We can date Hayek's skepticism toward the actions and motives of governments from this point.

He officially registered at New York University, where he began work on a Ph.D. thesis (never completed) on the question, "Is the function of money consistent with an artificial stabilization of purchasing power?" He attended one lecture by Thorstein Veblen, with whom he seems to have had nothing in common except having had malaria. What caught his interest were the newly developed techniques for the statistical analysis of economic time series, and the proposition then being talked about that the price level of an economy could be stabilized through monetary control by the central bank. The latter led to a study of the Federal Reserve system and U.S. monetary policy; the former to a new career on his return to Vienna.

The statistical methods then being developed in the United States under the leadership of Wesley Clair Mitchell were notable for the sophistication of their mathematical techniques, then unknown to European economists, and for the absence of any explanatory theory. Mitchell was hostile to any analysis that smacked of abstraction, having adopted a pragmatic institutionalist approach that owed something to the German historical school against which Carl Menger had inveighed.

The American approach to economic problems was to search for facts. The U.S. economy had been cursed by boom-and-bust cycles that defied prevention and/or explanation, however many facts were discovered. The boom phase of what would prove to be the most disastrous of these cycles was then under way. Mitchell had published his monumental work on business cycles in 1913 and had founded the National Bureau of Economic Research in New York. Hayek attended his lectures at Columbia University.

The Americans' effort to compare similar economic changes— changes in the price of corn or cotton, for example—over periods of time rested on an assumption (that is, assuming as fact that which remained to be demonstrated) that there were historical regularities in economic causes and effects. The pragmatic approach attempted to evade the epistemological necessity for a theory or hypothesis of the causes of economic changes, without which the significance of facts could not be recognized. In short, there would be no way to tell causes from effects.

Hayek's response to this approach was not to dismiss the possibility of regularities which the statistical investigations of the Americans appeared to be turning up, but to develop a theory which would explain them. After his return to Austria he wrote two significant papers, "Das intertemporale Gleichgewichtssystem der Preise und die Bewegungen des 'Geldwertes'" (1928) [Intertemporal Price Equilibrium and Movements in the Value of Money] and "Geldtheorie und Konjunkturtheorie" (1933)

[Monetary Theory and the Trade Cycle]. The latter was written to persuade German-speaking economists to consider monetary causes of industrial fluctuations, rather than the 'real' causes they believed must be found somewhere at the bottom of things.

Yet the pragmatism of the American approach did not conceal the true objective of their statistical studies, which was to find a way to control the economic events under investigation. It was only much later that Hayek understood the full impact, the dangerous presumption in the position he first heard enunciated in one of Mitchell's lectures. Hayek later termed it 'constructivism': the formula that, since man has himself created the institutions of society and civilization, he must also be able to alter them at will so as to satisfy his desires or wishes.

Luckily for Hayek, notification that he had received one of the first Rockefeller grants, which would have enabled him to extend his stay in the United States, did not arrive until after he had set sail for his return to Vienna in the spring of 1924. He returned to his job at the *Abrechnungsamt,* to participation in Mises's *Privatseminar,* and to discussions with Mises about the methods of economic research he had studied in the United States. Mises set about to secure funding for an institute devoted to business cycle research, and by January 1927 they were able to establish the *Österreichische Konjunkturforschungsinstitut* with Hayek as director. And staff. For the first years he wrote single-handedly most of the reports of the institute.

This occupation did not prevent his other writing, but it did leave him less time for it. Nonetheless he began a thorough study of the history of monetary theory (which, owing to later circumstances, was not published until it appeared in translation in 1991 in vol. 3 of his Collected Works). An unforeseen benefit of this study, from which Hayek acquired a detailed knowledge of British monetary theory and practice, would be to help him obtain a professorship in London.

Another engagement with American ideas had an even more improbable effect. Widely publicized in the United States at the time were proposals by Foster and Catchings which Hayek has described as variations on 'underconsumption' theories of economic cycles. Hayek argued against such theories in his initial lectures as a *Privatdozent* in Vienna. His published essay "Gibt es einen Widersinn des Sparens?" (1929) (later translated into English as "The Paradox of Saving") came to the attention of Lionel (later Lord) Robbins, who invited Hayek to give a series of lectures at the London School of Economics. So successful were the lectures, and the ensuing partnership with Robbins, that Hayek remained in England to become the Tooke professor at the LSE. He has written an engaging memoir of his intellectual life in these two decades, "The Economics of the 1920s as Seen from Vienna" (published in vol. 4 of his Collected Works) and "The Economics of the 1930s as Seen from London" (to be found in vol. 9).

England, the LSE, and Keynes

The early 1930s, Hayek wrote in that memoir, "appear to me much the most exciting period in the development of economic theory during this century. . . . The years between 1931, when I went to London, and say 1936 or 1937, seem to me to mark a high point and the end of one period in the history of economic theory and the beginning of a new and very different one." In 1936 Hayek delivered his presidential address before the London Economic Club. It was published the following year as the essay "Economics and Knowledge." In 1936 John Maynard Keynes published *The General Theory of Employment, Interest, and Money*.

The impact of the change in economic theory cannot be understood apart from the political and cultural upheavals of the time. But even a brief account of the history of the period is beyond the scope of this introduction. If it is difficult for us to comprehend how much the world changed in this century, it was even more difficult for those who experienced the great upheavals to understand their significance.

Utterly forgotten now, except in the annals of England, is that the history of the nineteenth century was preeminently the history of the British empire, the greatest empire the world had known. It was dominant as a political, military, and economic power. To a large extent, classical economic theory was the economics of the British empire.

The Great War had severely weakened the financial underpinnings of the empire. The huge shifts of capital and liquidations of monetary reserves required to pay for the war were unthinkable in terms of any of the transactional relations that economic theory could account for. *Force majeure* is not in the economist's lexicon.

Hayek notes that John Maynard Keynes had become a hero on the European continent by writing *The Economic Consequences of the Peace*. Keynes argued that the defeated Germany (and the Germans had come to regard themselves as not so much defeated as betrayed into a punitive armistice) could not pay the reparations which France demanded without exports at a level which the other powers would not tolerate. Whatever the accuracy of the figures which Keynes used to bolster his argument, the predicament was real. While governments argued, Germany and Austria succumbed to starvation and hyperinflation.

The British government adopted two positions that would prove mutually incompatible and eventually ruinous. His Majesty's Government would not surrender any claims for reparations unless the United States forgave its claims against Britain. And Britain, after furious debate, returned to a gold standard with the pound at its prewar parity. The City of London would soon find itself unable to balance the internal and external claims against it. Britain could no longer afford to be the lender of last resort to half the world.

Keynes played Cassandra in this debate with his pamphlet "The Economic Consequences of Mr. Churchill." He failed to carry the day.

With Hayek in London, Lionel Robbins had set forth on a grand design: to establish a unified tradition in economic theory and abolish all separate 'schools.' Hayek's first lectures, later revised and published as *Prices and Production*, and his review of Keynes's *Treatise on Money* were critical efforts in the campaign. Keynes's rejoinder was to attack *Prices and Production*. The lines were drawn.

The debate over theoretical questions was overtaken by events. The industrial world was sinking into depression, deeper and more intractable than any economist could have imagined. For economists who had begun to question the viability of their discipline in the face of Marxist attack, the strategy laid out in *The General Theory* proved to be a tactical winner. By identifying what appeared to be an imperfect link between savings and investment (which Hayek recognized as a sophisticated version of an underconsumption theory), Keynes opened the door for government intervention in monetary and fiscal measures, while still preserving the conceptual apparatus and justifications of a theory of general equilibrium.

The world, in any event, had stopped relying on any sort of economic theory. The shape of the next two decades, and beyond, was being forged in Germany by Hjalmar Schacht, who was devising a system of currency controls and directed investment that would be the first and last resort of every desperate government from then on.

By this time Hayek's view of economic cycles appeared to be utterly *hors de combat*. He made one heroic attempt (*The Pure Theory of Capital*) to integrate his recasting of Austrian capital theory with developments in neo-classical theory—the point where Keynesian theory was weakest—but by then the Second World War was under way and no one was listening.

Years later—when it had been clearly demonstrated that the success of any Keynesian program rested on the astuteness of political decisions which would never be forthcoming and not on the theoretical propositions of Keynes's work, which were at best muddled and at worst contradictory—Hayek stated that it was one of his greatest regrets that he did not mount an effective criticism of Keynes's ideas. In retrospect it is doubtful whether any criticisms would have prevailed, since the shift to Keynes and his eventual triumph was moved by cultural and political changes and not by the persuasiveness of the theoretical argument, the results of which were never empirically demonstrated owing to the outbreak of the Second World War. At the start of that war Hayek and Keynes found themselves in agreement over the way in which the cost of the war could be met to prevent inflation and the speculative excesses that had developed during the First World War. Their scheme relied on enforced savings which would be returned at the end of the war. At that point, Keynes had ceased to be a Keynesian.

The rapid changing of Keynes's mind was one of the main reasons Hayek gives for not attacking the *General Theory*. Keynes was almost notorious for this habit. There is a reported exchange with Churchill, who, during negotiations with the United States over postwar financial institutions, sent Keynes a note, "Am coming around to your point of view," only to get back the answer, "Sorry to hear it; have started to change my mind."

Economics and Knowledge

In retrospect Hayek thought that his essay "Economics and Knowledge," together with the later papers on the same subject, was his most original contribution to economics. It is also the answer to Keynes. The implications of Hayek's argument demolish both the logical and empirical assumptions which underlie the economics of the positivists, econometrics, and any attempt to create a "macroeconomics." This is a sweeping claim that fairness to Hayek requires, but one which I will not defend here.

Hayek's view of the market stands as the one informative statement of the problem of social organization. As he wrote in this seminal essay,

> How can the combination of fragments of knowledge existing in different minds bring about results which, if they were to be brought about deliberately, would require a knowledge on the part of the directing mind which no single person can possess? To show that in this sense the spontaneous actions of individuals will, under conditions which we can define, bring about a distribution of resources which can be understood as if it were made according to a single plan, although nobody has planned it, seems to me indeed an answer to the problem which has sometimes been metaphorically described as that of the 'social mind.' (*Individualism and Economic Order*, p. 54.)

In these sentences Hayek has engaged the problem—how order creates itself—that he had first glimpsed while attempting in his early psychological essay to account for the transformation of sensation into perception. There the problem emerged in the context of human physiology and psychology. Here the problem emerges in the context of human social organization, where the limits of individual knowledge are transcended.

He had gained confidence in his new approach from two sources. One, oddly enough, came from his first inspiration in economics, Carl Menger. In 1934 Hayek had accepted the welcome task of editing a new edition of Menger's writings that was sponsored by the London School of Economics. In the course of this work Hayek gave serious attention, perhaps for the first time, to Menger's writings on the methodology of the social sciences. There, as Hayek noted later, "the conception of the spontaneous generation of institutions is worked out more beautifully than in any other book I know." Hayek's other discovery was *Logik der Forschung* [The Logic of Scientific Discovery] by Karl Popper, published in 1934. Though fellow Viennese, Popper and Hayek had not met. They responded to the same intellectual influences—Mach, the logical positivists, Marx and Freud—with a largely compatible approach. Popper's argument against the logical foundations of induction offered Hayek an approach to empiricism which he found useful in his own attack on the assumptions of positivist economics.

By 1938 Hayek had become a British subject and, travelling on a British passport, managed to visit Austria once more before the outbreak of war. Some vital part of Hayek's heart and soul never left Vienna. It was Vienna itself which would change irrevocably; after the *Anschluss* the creative and intellectual energy that had been so powerful a force in molding this century was dispersed throughout the world. Most who could escape went to the United States. Popper went first to New Zealand, until Hayek was able to bring him to London after the war.

In manner and temperament Hayek felt entirely at home in England. Or rather he felt entirely at home in the England which still preserved much of the character of the nineteenth century. In such figures of that earlier time as Henry Thornton and Sir Leslie Stephen, and even more so in Lord Acton, he recognized kindred spirits. Not so surprising, perhaps, that Hayek would realize the necessity of the social institutions of manners and morals, law and language, for the evolution of civilization. He later described himself as a Burkean Whig.

Sharing the sport of mountaineering gave him an appreciation of the character of Sir Leslie Stephen. Hayek met a descendant of Henry Thornton, E. M. Forster, as a fellow member of the Reform Club. When the LSE moved to Cambridge to escape the bombing of London, Keynes found Hayek rooms. At Cambridge Hayek was able to share his interest in monetary history with Sir John Clapham. And yet when the war started he was quietly but definitely excluded. His faithful friend and ally, Lionel Robbins, went with Keynes into government service. Most of the leading economists were taken up with war planning. Keynes would so exhaust himself that he would barely survive the end of the war.

War and the Road to Serfdom

By 1940 no thoughtful person anywhere in the world could keep from wondering what had gone wrong. How could the promise of eighteenth century enlightenment, and the ethical and material progress of the nineteenth century, have led to the barbaric violence of the twentieth? Hayek took hold of the question from three perspectives: economic theory, psychological and biological theories, and historical investigation of philosophical and political ideas.

Beginning with essays that were later collected in *The Counter-Revolution of Science* and *Individualism and Economic Order*, Hayek took great pains to demonstrate how the character of the facts, the basic subject matter of the social sciences, had been misconstrued and misused through the attempted application of methods drawn from the physical sciences. The controlling fallacy was that it was possible to isolate sufficient instances of some phenomenon such that some general law as to the cause of the phenomenon could be ascertained. Hayek did not directly attack the inductive fallacy at work but rested his criticism on the subjective (thus indeterminate) character of the so-called facts of the social sciences. This subjective nature of the object of inquiry meant, so it might be argued, that those whose behavior submitted to general laws held ideas about the consequences of that behavior which were unpredictable. These ideas could not be reduced to 'facts' in the physical sense. The search for general laws of human behavior—conducted through a misconstruction of the logical relationship that pertains between a physical law and any consequence of that law and then applied to a study of history—was motivated by the ambition to control social institutions. Hayek termed the misapplication of the methods of the physical sciences to the social sciences 'scientism' and its use as a justification for controlling society 'constructivism.' This misapplication was the abuse of reason that he traced to Descartes and specifically to Auguste Comte.

The illusion that man could control his environment had been fostered by two great inventions: the steam engine and artificial dyes. The principles at work in the first—the behavior of gasses in a given volume—expanded the mechanistic concept of equilibrium which came to dominate economic theory. Meanwhile, the discovery of the process for manufacturing artificial dyes led to the belief that the very structure of physical matter could be altered and shaped to fit human designs. Eureka: Alchemy had become chemistry. As Henry Adams observed, the power of the turbine had displaced the power of the Virgin Mary to drive men's vision: Skyscrapers would be built, not cathedrals.

The abstract division, the front between the products of nature and the products of design—Aristotle's dichotomy—was becoming occluded. The possibility of designing more 'rational' institutions for human society was used as the lever, the driving wedge to weaken the legitimacy of existing institutions. Hayek's argument against the possibility of rationally designing social and economic organization rested on his demonstration that the knowledge of individual events that such a design would require was unobtainable because of the complexity of the events; and even if it were obtainable, the unforeseen consequences that social actions engender would defeat the design which produced them.

Hayek wrote the first two essays of his studies on the abuse of reason in a "state of intensive concentration with which [he] reacted to [his] impotence against the continuous disruptions of falling bombs." His safety in Cambridge did nothing to lessen his sense of despair over what was happening to the world. Frightening as the bombs were, perhaps even more alarming were the changes going on in the minds of economists and philosophers in the still-free world. It was an experience rather like a science-fiction story, something like the invasion of the body-snatchers. Outwardly, people seemed to be who they had been. Inside, they were captured by an alien spirit. The irony was that Hayek was treated as an alien while he, increasingly alone, preserved a devotion to that very liberty being fought for against the Axis powers.

The alien spirit which had captured intellectuals in both Britain and the United States was a belief that socialism was inevitable. Those who urged this view on their fellows misunderstood, perhaps chose to misunderstand, the source of the totalitarian aggression of Germany and Russia, arguing that one was the reaction against the other; that National Socialism in Germany was not, in fact, socialism, but a kind of hypercapitalist reaction to communism.

Hayek wrote about the sources of his own interpretation of events in his introduction to *The Road to Serfdom:* "Thus, by moving from one country to another, one may sometimes twice watch similar phases of intellectual development. The senses have then become peculiarly acute. When one hears for a second time opinions expressed or measures advocated which one has first met twenty or twenty-five years ago, they assume a new meaning as symptoms of a definite trend. They suggest, if not the necessity, at least the probability, that developments will take a similar course."

Hayek took pains to state that in *The Road to Serfdom* he was not making an historicist argument; he was not making claims for a logical inevitability. His argument was that if the totalitarian trends inherent in the process of central planning of economies and societies were not checked, the fate of Russia and Germany would be the fate of Britain. To put it in blunt contemporary parlance: He was making a wake-up call.

To intellectuals who were more favorably disposed toward socialism, Hayek's warning sounded like a rude noise. One such, Rudolf Carnap, the leading logical positivist philosopher, then safely resident in the United States, wrote to Karl Popper to chastise him for praising *The Road to Serfdom* "which, of course, [Carnap said he] had not read." Keynes wrote to Hayek to praise the book, claiming to be in perfect agreement with it, but justified his actions out of the hubris that all intellectuals who acquire power in the world sooner or later fall prey to:

> What we need therefore, in my opinion, is not a change in
> our economic programmes, which would only lead in practice
> to disillusion with the results of your philosophy; but perhaps
> even the contrary, namely, an enlargement of them. Your
> greatest danger ahead [here Cassandra Keynes is at it again]
> is the probable practical failure of the application of your

philosophy in the United States in a fairly extreme form. No, what we need is the restoration of right moral thinking—a return to proper moral values in our social philosophy. If only you could turn your crusade in that direction you would not look or feel quite so much like Don Quixote. I accuse you of perhaps confusing a little bit the moral and the material issues. Dangerous acts can be done safely in a community which thinks and feels rightly, which would be the way to hell if they were executed by those who think and feel wrongly.

As time went on, the fact that Britain and the United States did not become totalitarian was cited to discredit Hayek's warning. His critics did not realize how the experiences of the war had inured people to the loss of freedom; their argument seemed to be that as long as planning took place outside forced-labor camps there was no danger.

The animus of the planners, and their confusion, is demonstrated in the round-table discussion in this volume, republished as a dramatic reenactment of the anger and incomprehension that was vented on Hayek personally. As one of the participants challenged him: "I have not found that our planning was leading toward serfdom but rather toward freedom, toward emancipation, toward the higher levels of human personality" (see p. 110). Blinded by their 'special insight" into the higher levels of human personality, those who would design the world cannot see the peril they may cause: They cannot see that their plans, *even if they succeed*, will produce unintended, unforeseen consequences—which may open the door to the unscrupulous opportunist while the rest of us, who have surrendered our initiative to the planners, are left helpless. Perhaps it is an innate paradox of human nature: However well-meaning, however selfless, planners may be, a selfish opportunist may have the talents we need to meet the unexpected, to adapt to forces that will always be beyond our control.

Hayek clearly understood that while we may safely plan in the small (in the short run), we cannot plan in the large (in the long run). Keynes criticized Hayek for not being able to draw the line between these two possibilities. But Keynes did not grasp that the very unpredictability of where the line will fall augurs ill for the best-laid plans, not for the adaptations of the market. (Keynes wrote to Hayek, "The line of argument you yourself take depends on the very doubtful assumption that planning is not more efficient. Quite likely from the purely economic point of view it is efficient.") The complexity of the task of providing for the long run requires the spontaneously responsive systems that free markets provide.

In his own life, Hayek would always encounter the difficulty of the task. As he writes, "I have often been acutely aware of the fact that—I believe more than most other people—my thought was directed wholly to the future. I seem very early to have lost the capacity quietly to enjoy the present, and what made life interesting to me were my plans for the future—satisfaction consisted largely in having done what I had planned to do, and mortification mainly that I had not carried out my plans" (see p. 138). Perhaps, to paraphrase Keynes, in the long run we are all mortified.

It is yet another of the anomalies of Hayek's character that this great political philosopher seems to have been a terrible politician. He sensed that the case he had to argue in *The Road to Serfdom* would never find a hearing among the professional economists and civil servants, the academic philosophers and social scientists, to whom it was really addressed: the socialists of all parties. He took his case directly to the wider public, taking great care to make the style of *The Road to Serfdom* as readable as he could manage. There he succeeded far beyond his expectations.

No philosopher with a political instinct, for whom truth serves the given objective and not vice versa, could have written as Hayek did in *The Road to Serfdom* (p. 165):

> This interaction of individuals, possessing different knowledge and different views, is what constitutes the life of thought. The growth of reason is a social process based on the existence of such differences. It is of its essence that its results cannot be predicted, that we cannot know which views will assist this growth and which will not—in short, that this growth cannot be governed by any views which we now possess without at the same time limiting it. To 'plan' or 'organize' the growth of mind, or, for that matter, progress in general, is a contradiction in terms. The idea that the

human mind ought 'consciously' to control its own development confuses individual reason, which alone can 'consciously control' anything, with the interpersonal process to which its growth is due. By attempting to control it, we are merely setting bounds to its development and must sooner or later produce a stagnation of thought and a decline of reason.

At the start of the defense build-up in Britain, the labor unions and the Labour Party discovered they had regained the political leverage they had lost in the 1920s after the General Strike. They used this political power to veto the proposal which Hayek and Keynes had put together to manage the extraordinary financial requirements for paying for armament production. Keynes and Hayek's plan relied on enforced savings—to be returned after the war—to reduce civilian demand, thus allowing the market to respond to government demand in the most efficient way. Labour suspected that all the sacrifices would be theirs and would have none of it. The result was ever-increasing control of every aspect of life: rationing of virtually all commodities; wage, price and rent controls; foreign-exchange and capital controls. All of these controls would remain long after the war had ended.

The political lesson, which the socialists learned and the Keynesians did not, is that if a government guarantees demand for labor through its own direct spending, a government loses any means for countering the demands of labor. The political conceit of the Keynesians was to believe they could ride that tiger. But the smile was on the face of the tiger.

Hayek made one more proposal to arrest the growing powers of government. He proposed a new currency standard to replace the suspended gold standard based on a fixed, internationally traded basket of commodities. The proposal was submitted to the international monetary conference at Bretton Woods in 1944. Keynes, of course, led the British delegation and was largely responsible for the resulting agreement. Lionel Robbins went with him. Hayek was not invited. His proposal was not considered.

Published in 1944, *The Road to Serfdom* found a wide audience in Britain. It created a sensation in the United States, and in

1946 Hayek was invited to give a lecture tour. He was given his fifteen minutes of fame.

Word of the book reached Germany through former prisoners of war who read the condensed version which had been printed in *Reader's Digest*. The occupying powers had banned the publication of *The Road to Serfdom* in Germany with the official declaration that it might impair good relations with the U.S.S.R. Despite the ban, excerpts from the book circulated in Germany in typewritten copies. When Hayek later read some of these typescripts, he found to his amazement that sometimes the typists had added passages of their own.

The academic economists and social scientists to whom the book had been addressed dismissed *The Road to Serfdom* as a 'popular' book which was beneath their notice. Hayek was shunned.

Exile

Hayek was about to learn a lesson that academics—unlike politicians, athletes, and actors—are slow to learn: Timing is everything. Much of his work in economic theory had addressed the difficulty of introducing time factors into equilibrium processes. But in most economic theory the critical factors of time in human relationships—what occurs when, and how long the time between cause and effect may be—are waved off stage or off the page with blithe references to expectations, risk, and outcomes. Diligent planners of the war effort—including John Kenneth Galbraith and Richard Nixon—who rationed and requisitioned and froze anything they could count, were not then, nor perhaps even now, prepared to concede that all their efforts would have been for naught but for the timely discovery of radar and the breaking of codes, and the timely failure of Germany to find substitutes for wool and oil on the eastern front. Reading, for example, the witty self-congratulatory (or deprecating) accounts by Galbraith (*A Life in Our Times*), is it not impossible to believe that if a mind that acute could not run an economy successfully, how could a free market born of unfettered and untutored behavior be better?

The answer lies in the means that those with mutual interests find to communicate with one another. Even the dullest of individuals has knowledge of his or her own circumstances that may prove to be valuable to others. The evolution of the means of social organization—the result of human action but not of human design—is both the actual and theoretical answer to the economic problem of coordinating the needs and plans of millions of dispersed participants. Hayek traced the origins of this idea through Adam Smith, David Hume, and Adam Ferguson to Bernard Mandeville: "The worst of all the multitude, Did something for the common good."

We who are not Galbraiths need simple rules of conduct to follow and simple means to petition our betters. Over time this need generates the rules of language, law, manners, and morals. The use of money and the exchange of goods and services in open markets seem to develop as simply as the flocking of pigeons to spilled corn.

Of these aspects or institutions of human intercourse, manners are often overlooked, but these acquired habits—mode of address, style of dress, the boundaries of privacy and thus property—may be most important in enabling people to live and work together. Hayek gives a perfect example of this by way of explaining why he felt so at home in England: "The way you break off a conversation. You don't say, 'Oh, I'm sorry; I'm in a hurry.' You become slightly inattentive and evidently concerned with something else; you don't need a word" (see p. 100). Manners are inseparable from language—the gesture, the tone of voice—and blend almost imperceptibly into morals, which blend altogether too perceptibly into laws.

Hayek had been fortunate in his timing in his professional life. He was not so fortunate in his personal life. He had fallen in love when he was quite young with a woman who was a cousin. Through some misunderstanding of his intentions, she had married someone else. Hayek also married, moved to England, and became a father. After the war he visited Austria to see the family members who had remained behind (he encountered his cousin Wittgenstein on the train on a similar errand) and learned that his first love felt she was again free to marry him. He decided that no matter what the immediate pain and cost to him and his family, he had no choice but to seek a divorce.

Given what Hayek then suffered in his situation in London

and with some of his closest associates, it is curious that he never wrote of the other aspect of a moral tradition: its power to exclude and to isolate. Publishing *The Road to Serfdom* had cut him off from most professional economists. The scandal of his divorce would cut him off from much of his former society.

He did what other outcasts have done before him. He went to America and wrote a constitution of liberty.

"It is probable that it was at the beginning of this time that they had become aware of the scandalous talk about them, had learnt to exercise caution, and that they withdrew almost completely from society. . . . The situation and the natural inclinations of both parties must have combined from the beginning to make the position of women and their position in marriage one of the main topics of common interest." The words are Hayek's, writing about John Stuart Mill and Harriet Taylor (*John Stuart Mill and Harriet Taylor*, p. 110). Hayek's study of Mill had grown out of the historical research he had begun on the abuse of reason. His edition of the letters of John Stuart Mill and Harriet Taylor, subtitled "their friendship and subsequent marriage," is fascinating on several accounts. It is an important document for Hayek's contention that the drift toward socialism in England began with Taylor and Mill. But it also shows Hayek completely at home in his adopted country of England, combining historical, scholarly, and antiquarian talents (he was a great book collector) to produce a record of a relationship that goes to the heart of English culture. It is also fascinating because Hayek writes about the very personal roots of human relationships; the content, as it were, of some of the subjective values that move economic and political developments. These are complex facts that are not reducible—in the positivist methodology—to common measurement.

In 1954 Hayek received a grant from the Guggenheim Foundation which allowed him and his wife to spend seven months retracing the journey Mill had made through Italy and Greece exactly one hundred years earlier. They made one departure from the Mill itinerary: to Egypt, where Hayek delivered the lectures on "The Political Ideal of the Rule of Law." On his return to Chicago in the fall of 1955, the plan for *The Constitution of Liberty* stood clearly before him.

It is indeed a truth, which all the great apostles of freedom outside the rationalistic school have never tired of emphasizing, that freedom has never worked without deeply ingrained moral beliefs and that coercion can be reduced to a minimum only where individuals can be expected as a rule to conform voluntarily to certain principles. There is an advantage in obedience to such rules not being coerced, not only because coercion as such is bad, but because it is, in fact, often desirable that rules should be observed only in most instances and that the individual should be able to transgress them when it seems to him worthwhile to incur the odium which this will cause. It is also important that the strength of the social pressure and of the force of habit which insures their observance is variable. It is this flexibility of voluntary rules which in the field of morals makes gradual evolution and spontaneous growth possible, which allows further experience to lead to modifications and improvements.

So Hayek wrote in *The Constitution of Liberty* (pp. 62–63). The book was published on February 9, 1960.

The Sensory Order

Hayek was offered a position at the University of Chicago. John Nef recalled the circumstances (*Search for Meaning*, p. 37):

My visit to England, where I met T. S. Eliot and Friedrick Hayek in London, enabled me to make those two important appointments to the Committee on Social Thought. Hayek accepted a permanent chair he was destined to hold for almost fifteen years. The Economics Department welcomed his connection with Social Thought, although the economists had opposed his appointment in Economics four years before largely because they regarded his *Road to Serfdom* as too popular a work for a respectable scholar to perpetrate. It was all right to have him at the University of Chicago so long as he wasn't identified with the economists.

Hayek joined the faculty in October 1950 as professor of social and moral science. He did not come empty-handed. He brought with him the first draft of a manuscript entitled "What Is Mind?"

As he later explained, "After *The Road to Serfdom*, I felt that I had so discredited myself professionally, I didn't want to give offense again. I wanted to be accepted in the scientific community. To do something purely scientific and independent of my economic view" (see p. 152). It is an awkward moment in intellectual history. Ready at last to disclose his response to Aristotle, Locke, and Hume, Hayek finds himself in the New World, which, having demonstrated its mastery of obstacles to survival to its own satisfaction, has no patience for epistemological difficulties.

Hayek returned to the problem he had first encountered thirty years before in the *Analysis of Sensations* by Ernst Mach. Hayek had set himself the task of tracing sensations through neural impulses to the brain where they become perceptions which seem to correspond in some way to 'reality.' By the third draft, the manuscript of "What Is Mind?" had become *The Sensory Order*. He described the development of his concepts in "The Sensory Order After 25 Years" (p. 289):

> What I had from the beginning been unable to swallow was the conception that a sensory fibre could carry, or a nerve cell store, those distinctive attributes that we know mental phenomena to possess—know not only by introspection but equally from our observation of other people's behavior. The result of my earlier studies had been a clear perception of the fact that these mental properties could be determined by the place of the impulse in a system of relations between all the neurons through which impulses were passed. This led me to interpret the central nervous system as an apparatus of multiple classification or, better, as a process of continuous and simultaneous classification and constant reclassification on many levels (of the legion of impulses proceeding in it at any moment), applied in the first instance to all sensory perception but in principle to all the kinds of mental entities, such as emotions, concepts, images, drives, etc., that we find to occur in the mental universe.

The conception that Hayek attacks—that "experience begins with the reception of sensory data possessing constant qualities which either reflect corresponding attributes belonging to the perceived external objects, or are uniquely correlated with such attributes of the elements of the physical world" (*The Sensory Order*, p. 165)—begins with Aristotle's insistence that we learn the 'essence' of things and comes down to us through John Locke's maxim of empiricism: *Nihil est intellectu quod non antea fuerit in sensu* [Nothing is in the mind which is not placed there by the senses]. The route that Hayek chooses to mount his attack runs parallel to Kant's and from time to time seems to merge with it.

Prior to Mach, one discovers, there were orchids in Hayek's life, and it is that 'prior to' which is the key to the sensory order. As Hayek tells us, in following the interest of his botanist father, he "also started my own herbarium and even began a monograph on *Orchis condigera*. . . . Systematic botany with its puzzle of the existence of clearly defined classes proved a useful education. But my interest gradually shifted from botany to paleontology and the theory of evolution . . . then Father was perceptive enough to see that my mind was more theoretical than it was in taxonomy" (see pp. 43–44).

The classifications which the mind acquires to sort out undifferentiated sensations stem from prior experience. "Every sensation, even the 'purest' must therefore be regarded as an interpretation of an event in the light of the past experience of the individual or the species." The use of a prior classification to determine the 'sense' of a sensation differs from Kant's use of an a priori category in that Hayek's classifications emerge within the process of perception itself and do not remain fixed. They are not equivalent to a principle or axiom. And therein lies the link—or "linkage," in his terminology—with the development of spontaneous orders.

"The reclassification which is thus performed by the mind is a process similar to that through which we pass in learning to read aloud a language which is not spelled phonetically. We learn to give identical symbols different values according as they appear in combination with different other symbols, and to recognize different groups of symbols as being equivalent without even noticing the individual symbols" (*The Sensory Order*, p. 169).

Was the book a failure? Since publication it seems to have gone largely unread; even Hayek scholars who are aware of its importance observe the obligation to read it more in the breach. Initially there were positive reviews, but even in the most appreciative, one can spot the beginning of difficulties that lay ahead for the work. As Hayek observed many years later, "So far as psychology is concerned, I am really a ghost from the nineteenth century."

The modern trend toward specialization had accelerated, particularly in American universities. Hayek's argument in *The Sensory Order* struck a lethal blow to the behaviorism then dominant in academic psychology. Hayek was passed over by what would prove to be an unfavorable evolution in the style and content of academic work in epistemology and psychology. (Outside the university, the popular exploration of mental phenomena went on in the same wildly intuitive way as always. Had Hayek written of 'extra-sensory' elements instead of 'pre-sensory,' he might well have been invited on another lecture tour.)

"When an expert such as Hayek, however reputed in the socio-economic field, writes a treatise on perception, his transgression will meet with many a raised eyebrow or blank stare," wrote one reviewer, reflecting that link between manners and language. Even the most positive review, from Edwin G. Boring in the *Scientific Monthly*, took Hayek to task for one conspicuous failure:

> Even when he is right (and that, I should say, is most of the time) you wish he would do a reasonable share of the work in connecting up his thought with that of his predecessors. Physical theories of mind and consciousness, and relational theories, are not new, and one would like to be shown, not merely the content of Hayek's mind, but his theory in the perspective of the history of scientific thought about these matters. Nevertheless, let me add to my reminder that Hayek's views have antecedents, that I feel sure that no one has done this particular job nearly so well.

In 1956, at a celebration of the twenty-fifth anniversary of the opening of the Social Science Research Building at the University of Chicago, Hayek delivered a lecture entitled "The Dilemma of Specialization." He could not help but plead his own case. "We certainly ought to feel nothing but admiration for the mature scholar who is willing to run the serious risk of disregarding all the boundaries of specialization in order to venture on tasks for which perhaps no man can claim full competence" (*Studies in Philosophy, Politics, and Economics*, p. 127).

The vital connection of *The Sensory Order* with the core of Hayek's economic and political theories becomes even more apparent in later essays, particularly "The Theory of Complex Phenomena" and "Rules, Perception and Intelligibility," which he wrote to expand the philosophical implications of *The Sensory Order*.

Arguments both for and against the efficacy of the central planning that socialism inevitably requires either stand or fall on the epistemological justification of the ability to predict the consequences of actions. As Hayek states clearly in his essay "Degrees of Explanation," "While it is evidently possible to predict precisely without being able to control, we shall clearly not be able to control developments further than we can predict the results of our action. A limitation of prediction thus implies a limitation of control, but not vice versa" (*Studies*, p. 18).

To account for the limitations of the ability to predict human actions, Hayek developed a theory of complex phenomena which admits of the possibility of the prediction of *patterns*— recurrent associations of a range of effects with limited causes— but not of the prediction of individual events within those patterns. What allows individuals and groups to function despite the limits of prediction is the evolution of rules of perception, which allow action that is unpredictable. An example is the rules of grammar which permit one to form statements, the meaning of any one of which is unpredictable.

In 1960 Hayek wrote to Popper about his emerging investigation: "Though I do not mean to concentrate mainly on methodology, The New Look at Economic Theory which I am taking and which may result in a book of that title inevitably began with an attempt to restate my views of the nature of economic theory, and the conception of higher level regularities which I then formed continues to occupy me and seems fruitful far beyond the field of economics." In fact, he had already written to Popper in 1952 about the beginnings of this investigation. Popper's main objection to *The Sensory Order* was that it constituted a causal theory of the mind, which Popper argued was not possible. Hayek replied:

> Would you regard what I call an "explanation of the principle only" a causal explanation or not? If your argument were intended merely to prove that we can never explain why at a particular moment such and such sensations, mental processes, etc., take place I should agree. If, on the other hand, you were intending to deny that it can be explained how

physical processes can be arranged in the general <u>kind</u> of order which is characteristic of mental phenomena, it would need a great deal to convince me. Of course, my analysis of a particular problem raises the most far-reaching philosophical problems. I am now for months puzzling about what just now seems to me the most general problem of all and which at the moment I describe for myself as the distinction between what we can say "within a system" and what we can say "about a system." I am convinced that this is a most important problem, since ever since I began to see it clearly I meet it constantly in all sorts of different connections, but though I have made some little headway it is one of the most difficult and elusive problems I have ever tackled.

Hayek was right on both counts. The problem of what we can say within a system and about a system is most important, and it is difficult and elusive. He made one valiant attempt to address the problem by beginning a paper on 'systems within systems.' When he found that no one could follow his discussion, he gave it up. For the second time in his life, Hayek abandoned his investigation into the nature of human understanding and turned to the study of law.

Hayek never felt entirely at home in Chicago. He kept a car garaged in Paris and with his wife returned to his beloved Alps whenever possible. He was growing increasingly deaf, which cut him off from conversations. He had given up going to the theater entirely. More troubling were the bouts of depression which he suffered, beginning in 1960.

He made an extended effort to reestablish a center in Vienna, to be called the Institute of Advanced Human Studies, for the kind of intellectual life that had vanished with the war and that he so missed. He, Popper, and Sir Ernst Gombrich were to be its central figures. But opposition from the University of Vienna discouraged potential sponsors, particularly the Ford Foundation, which established its own sort of center for its own sort of social science. Needless to say, it did not recreate the lost Vienna.

In the winter of 1961–62, Hayek received an offer of a professorship at the University of Freiburg (in Breisgau, Germany). The offer carried an attractive proposal for his eventual retirement, and he accepted. Except for an unhappy interlude at

Salzburg from 1969 to 1977, he remained in Freiburg for the rest of his life, spending his summers in the mountains at Obergurgl.

In 1973 the international financial apparatus which Keynes at Bretton Woods had convinced the Americans was needed to save the postwar world from another disaster—but which was really designed to stave off the financial ruin of Britain—collapsed. The value of sterling had already declined with the empire, and now the dollar, cut loose from the last vestige of the gold standard, would follow it. Though Keynesian nostrums were rapidly losing credibility in the face of simultaneous inflation and unemployment, the appeal of socialism showed no sign of weakening, particularly in the universities.

In 1974, F. A. Hayek was awarded the Nobel prize for economic science. The first reaction of many of the interested public was astonishment that he was still alive. Then, recalling that he once argued against the theories of Keynes, some of the public began to take an interest in what Hayek had to say. He gave them a cogent defense of a free market as a necessary foundation for a free society. He also offered them an argument for the denationalization of money that proposed that a free market be utilized to maintain the value of money. Since governments had proven themselves incapable of the job, Hayek's proposal was certainly not beyond consideration. But bankers had been creatures of government regulation for so long they had forgotten what a market was.

The market will prevail, however far underground it must go. Hayek's view of the market, of the spontaneous order of social institutions, does not need to be justified or enforced. It is the way life is. One need only wait. The walls always come down.

Looking Back

Not all the boundaries which separate us are as brutal and ugly as the Berlin Wall. Some are as simple as measuring in inches rather than millimeters; or a preference for Bach over rock. Yet everything changes. As Hayek has made clear, the task of economic theory is really to explain how we bring about an adaptation to what is unknowable. We should think, he says, of "economics as a stream instead of an equilibrating force, as we ought, quite literally, to think in terms of the factors that determine the movement of the flow of water in a very irregular bed" (see p. 147).

Hayek's achievement was to demonstrate that economic theory, like any theory of social behavior, is a theory of evolution. In so doing he has returned the study of social behavior to the course it had originally taken (the account of the evolution of languages by Sir William Jones, for example, and Adam Smith's *Wealth of Nations*), which inspired Darwin to explore the possibility of evolutionary change through natural selection as a way to explain the differentiation of living species. It is sometimes forgotten that Darwin believed that the adaptation demonstrated by the diversity of ericaceous shrubs in the sparse habitat of the moors could refute Malthus's dire predictions of populations expanding beyond their means of survival. Malthus had arrived at his dismal forecast of fecundity inevitably exceeding productivity through brooding at length on the fate of Ireland. Ricardo followed Malthus in accepting as the context for their discussion of economic theory an economy, conceptually much like an island, in which only the division of income can be in any way determined.

The convention of regarding the subject of economic theory as an entity much like an island persisted. Once a closed system is assumed, one can easily adopt an hypothesis of equilibrium borrowed from mechanics and, farther afield, physics. Predictability in such a system is the goal to be attained.

Alas for economic theory, it neglected Darwin's response to Malthus and followed Ricardo's. It would be a good many years before it could be observed that the precarious state of the Irish in Ireland was due to the unfortunate location of their island within the British Empire. In the United States their numbers were noticed, but it would take the fertility of more races than the Irish to overpopulate the New World. If the boundaries of a society, or a system, are altered, the behavior of the society is changed. These boundaries may be in any number of dimensions: time and space, of course, but the dimensions of knowledge are boundless; any change in our knowledge of any factor within or without the system requires a readjustment in the entire system.

The tragedy of the twentieth century has been the desolation of enormous populations, victims of what Hayek later termed the fatal conceit of socialism—the attempt to design and control the destiny of societies. Inevitably the failure of the design, in the Soviet Union and other communist societies, led to increasing control, which meant controlling knowledge by closing the society. It is not the fate of Ireland that, as Gibbon once wrote, is easier to deplore than to describe, but the fate of Cuba. No man is an island. Neither are islands.

Events have vindicated Hayek's argument. He attacked the constructivist ideal of controlling society by attacking the epistemological grounds for the possibility of control; he demonstrated that prediction of the responses to changes in economic and social systems is not possible. The evolution of spontaneous orders such as a free market is the means by which the diversity of adaptation to changing circumstances is made possible. Yet we must concede that Hayek's argument has been rarely heard. Social science faculties throughout the world have been more eager to teach Marx than Hayek. In the United States, economics has become the poor relation of mathematics.

Hayek's conclusions are now virtually undeniable. But an argument against prediction, that is, an argument against predicting *with certainty* a response to any change of social or economic conditions cannot at the same time demonstrate that any given attempt to plan or control a process will lead to failure. A plan might succeed out of sheer chance. We cannot predict that a plan will succeed, and we cannot predict that it won't. Thus the constructivists have a logical loophole. Hume lives.

The intellectual temptation has always been to close the loophole with the claim of the a priori validity of initial principles or premises. In a sea of uncertainty, the siren song is not Circe's but certainty's. Hayek sailed dangerously close to those rocks.

Looking Forward

Much of Hayek's writing has been a process of demarcation. He effectively demonstrated that most of our social institutions, such as language and money, were neither the products of deliberate human invention nor the elements of a natural environment, like wind and gravity. In *The Sensory Order* he demonstrated that the root of social order is an evolutionary process that proceeds from the classification of observed regularities to the formation of rules, which permit the interaction of the elements (dimensions) of a system in increasingly complex classifications. The evolutionary process is potentially open-ended, and the effects at any given time will be uncertain and unpredictable.

Hayek wrote *The Sensory Order* before the discovery of the structure of DNA. It is easier now to overlook the originality of his concept; it is also easier to understand it. The very basis of biological life, which evolves through genetic reproduction, follows Hayekian principles. The production of proteins which individual genes control is managed according to 'rules' analogous to the 'rules' of language. The possible combinations of a fixed number of amino acids can lead to countless numbers of proteins. These in turn interact in still more complex orders, forming organisms which in turn interact according to 'rules' of attraction and repulsion. At some point in this process we may be able to draw a line between the 'rules' of nature and the evolution of rules which produce spontaneous social orders. The problem is where we draw that line.

Hayek departed from Darwinian theory at two key points. He argues that the formation of spontaneous orders is through group selection (and not via individual mutation), and therefore that acquired characteristics must be transmissible. While these two propositions lead to critical explanations, they do not escape the main hazard of evolutionary theories, which is their tautological character. Survival is the only measure of successful adaptation, but survival provides no measure of the success of any adaptation. Nothing succeeds like survival, but here today, gone tomorrow. Just ask any dinosaur.

However, Hayek's theory suggests that it is the rules which survive, not necessarily the groups that form in accordance with those rules. I should state that this hypothesis can be inferred from Hayek's proposals; he does not state it explicitly. But if we adopt this measure to identify spontaneous orders (rather than natural or designed ones) a number of difficulties are avoided.

In his later work, Hayek slipped into using rules to justify a moral tradition that would prove superior for the survival of some (unspecified) groups over others. The danger of this argument is revealed in Keynes's response to *The Road to Serfdom*. Keynes argued that proper moral justification would permit the use of economic and political measures which would otherwise be unacceptable. Any attempt to justify a moral proposition opens one to a boomerang argument, a *tu quoque* which leaves one no defense against the argument that all such a priori principles, such as moral principles, are not rationally justifiable. At the other end, Hayek's claim that the mind cannot understand itself leads him to abandon reason in his own defense, even though he denies that appeal to his opponents.

If, however, we return to the hypothesis that it is the rules that survive, not necessarily the groups or individuals that adopt them, then the problem can be cast in different terms. Then the process of evolution—the equivalent of natural selection in species—becomes one of self-selection. This suggests that adaptations are successful when they allow larger numbers of individuals to communicate with one another and solve more of the problems of their environment. The group by which we measure the success of adopted rules is not a fixed population. The group of English-speakers, for example, varies from use to use and is never identical with any one population, say, the inhabitants of England. Adopting a theory of self-selection would go a long way to defuse some rising social conflicts, such as those surrounding the demands for multicultural biases in institutions and, at their worst, the 'ethnic cleansing' of certain tormented regions of the world. With a self-selecting basis for the formation of social organizations, an individual can participate in any number of spontaneous orders—languages, families, markets, religions—without sacrificing individual identity.

Perhaps the most fortunate irony of all in Hayek's life and work is that we have less reason to despair of reason because of him. His contention that the mind cannot understand itself derived from a major conclusion of *The Sensory Order:* "The proposition which we shall attempt to establish is that any apparatus of classification must possess a structure of a higher degree of complexity than is possessed by the objects which it classifies" (p. 185).

But he also understood that, with the possible exception of the human mind, there is no limit to the evolution of structures of greater and greater complexity. In his essay "Rules, Perception and Intelligibility," he came to understand that the problem was essentially the same as in certain other philosophical encounters with paradoxes and with the problem, as he had written to Popper, of what one can say about a system from within a system. Hayek abandoned his own investigations in this direction, but he opened a door, providing a context in which the next degree of complexity can be understood. Tarski's work on metalanguages and Bartley's work on rationality have already mapped some of the new territory.

It may take more political and economic disasters for the lesson to sink in, but we do seem to be learning that while the mind—reason—cannot impose a pattern of its own making on the world, it can discover and understand the patterns out of which life emerges. The thinkers in the emerging discipline of complex systems theory, even in that branch called artificial life (which may prove not to be an oxymoron), find themselves contemplating spontaneous orders of distinctly Hayekian character. Even on computers, unpredictable complex forms evolve from sets of simple rules.

Life, so these researchers are coming to understand, be it artificial or natural, exists on the edge of chaos. Hayek lives.

Stephen Kresge

PART ONE

Vienna–New York–Vienna

The earliest paternal ancestor of whom more than the bare name is known is my great-great-grandfather, Josef Hayek (1750–1830), who in 1789 obtained the minor title of nobility (the "von"), which the family since bears. His father Laurenz Hayek had served one of the great aristocratic landowners of Moravia at his estate near Brünn (Brno), but had died when his son Josef was not yet five years old. Josef Hayek followed the landowner to Vienna as secretary when he was appointed to high government office, and after returning with him to Moravia became steward of the estate. In this capacity Josef Hayek developed two new textile factories in Moravia and Lower Austria, which, in turn, led to the formation of two new villages. He eventually also became a partner in these factories and acquired a substantial fortune. This was a significant achievement in the Austria of 1789, and it was this that led Kaiser Josef II to ennoble him at the early age of thirty-nine. Josef von Hayek had it inserted into his patent of nobility that both his father and grandfather had served in the Silesian wars. Apart from this, alas, I know nothing of these earlier ancestors.

Josef's son, Heinrich, used his substantial inheritance to study law, then married a gifted singer, Franziska Zwierzina; became a civil servant in one of the ministries in Vienna, where he probably had to work for only two or three hours each morning; and spent a long, dignified, and comfortable life as a gentleman. His son, my grandfather Gustav von Hayek, born in Brünn, was first educated by private tutors and later attended an elegant and fashionable school in Vienna, the Theresianum, at that time still reserved to members of the nobility. But he left school prematurely, several months before he would have obtained the *matura* necessary to enter university. He became a naval officer, and indeed seems to have been a bit of a young naval dandy. The earliest photograph that is preserved shows him thus as a naval cadet in Venice, then a base of the Austrian fleet.

To the misfortune of Gustav, his expectations of a career in the navy were dashed. His father Heinrich somehow, late in life, while his son was in the navy, lost the fortune on which the family's comfortable existence depended. I do not know the details of this disaster, but much of the money appears to have been lost already in the 1860s, long before the crisis of 1873 when so many of the upper-middle class in Austria lost their fortunes; and the situation was later made worse for the son (after he had already married and started a family) in that he also failed to inherit, as he had expected, that portion of the original fortune which had gone to his maiden aunts. Thus my grandfather, whether from simple dissatisfaction with navy life or to afford to marry (something not easy to accomplish on the tiny salary of a junior naval officer), or for some other reason, decided, by the time he had reached his late twenties, also to quit the navy. I say "or for some other reason" because he seems to have led a rather flashy life in the navy, which would hardly have been possible to continue without a fortune, and because there was a story that I only dimly remember of how the young cadet had once appeared on the promenade with some irregular adornment to his uniform and was saved from a seemingly inevitable punishment only by the commanding admiral's appearing the next day with the same modification to his own uniform.

Gustav returned to his studies after some difficulties arising from his premature departure from *Gymnasium*, studied natural history and biology, and eventually became a schoolmaster, a professor at a *Gymnasium*. Some of his systematic works on biology became fairly well known. Very briefly he enjoyed hopes of higher prospects when as an ornithologist he engaged the interest of Crown Prince Rudolf and was charged by him with organizing the first international ornithological exhibition at Vienna in 1881. But these hopes were disappointed when the Crown Prince committed suicide in 1889. This biological inter-

est was continued by my father August Edler von Hayek, my
two younger brothers (one an anatomist and the other a chem-
ist), and reappeared in my daughter (an entomologist).

If my father's parents, however proud of their gentility and an-
cestry, lived in modest circumstances, my mother's parents, the
von Jurascheks—although from a "younger" family and en-
nobled over a generation later—were definitely upper-class
bourgeoisie and wealthier by far. My grandfather Franz von Juraschek had been a university professor and later a top-ranking
civil servant, with a scholarly background and international reputation as a statistician. He was able to support an appropriate
standard of life by what must have been a nice fortune of his
wife.

The von Jurascheks were housed in a magnificent, even gran-
diose, top-floor flat of ten rooms at Kärtnerstrasse 55, where
they kept at least three servants. This was undoubtedly one of
the most beautiful flats in Vienna, across the Kärtnerstrasse from
the opera and facing the Ringstrasse, in a building that was later,
in 1914, after my grandfather's death, torn down and replaced
by the new Hotel Bristol. My grandparents' flat was a second
home to me where I spent, apart from at least every other Sunday afternoon, longer periods when my parents were away on
occasional journeys or after my father's serious illness in the
autumn of 1912 or so. Since the youngest child of my grandfather's second marriage, my uncle Franz, was only four or five
years my senior, the family present at those Sunday gatherings
was large and would include a continuous range of ages from
my grandparents themselves to my youngest cousins.

My parents were exceedingly well suited to each other, and
their married life seemed (not only to me) one of unclouded
happiness. Although in the early years money must have been
scarce (the small salary of my father, just appointed *Armenarzt*
[municipal physician for the poor, the lowest rank of the Medical
Office of Health], was at first just about equalled by the income
from my mother's small fortune, the total amounting, I believe,
to something like $2,000 in 1898), they were, during most of
their life, fairly comfortably situated.

As soon as the earning of some extra money had ceased to be

a matter of great urgency, my father seems to have given up any serious attempts to build up a private practice, and, content to rise gradually in the hierarchy of the ministry of health, devoted all his spare time to his beloved botany. He always hoped someday to be able to give up medicine altogether for a full university chair in botany, but that day never came, and the "Professor" was never more than the honorary title usually conferred on a *Privatdozent* of several years' standing. But while this unfulfilled ambition was a grief to him (and probably did much to make me regard a university chair as the most desirable of all positions I might attain), his scientific output was considerable, and in his particular field, plant geography (which today would be called ecology), he was highly respected by his fellows. His remarkable memory enabled him to acquire a quite exceptional knowledge of plants, and he himself used to remark, rather regretfully, that he was more or less the last botanist who regarded it as his business to recognize most plants on inspection.

During the last years of his life, my father had become a kind of social center for the botanists of Vienna, who met at regular intervals at our flat. He died relatively early, in his fifty-seventh year, of a kidney disease resulting from a severe blood poisoning (the result of a blister on his foot during a botanical excursion in Oststeiermarkt), of which he had nearly died some fifteen years earlier. My mother [Felicitas] died in 1967 in her ninety-third year.

My parents, though they had never formally left the ancestral Roman Catholic church, held no religious beliefs. Though they were no longer fiercely anti-religious (as I suspect my paternal grandfather was, along with so many of the scientists of his generation), all positive dogma was for them a superstition of the past. They never took me to church. And though as part of my general education I was, soon after I had begun to read for pleasure, given a child's Bible, it disappeared mysteriously when I got too interested in it.

There was of course religious instruction at school, and in the *Gymnasium* there was semi-compulsory attendance at mass on Sunday. The legitimacy of this pressure was always doubtful, and whenever a Sunday excursion (quite regular in the family on fine days in spring and summer) interfered, we boys just did not attend, which led to frequent friction with the school authorities. Only for a short time during the first two years of the *Gymnasium*, that is, at about the age of ten or eleven, did I develop strong religious feeling under the influence of a persuasive teacher. And I remember distinctly the anguish of the belief of having sinned between confession and first communion next morning. But this phase lasted only briefly. By the age of fifteen, I had convinced myself that nobody could give a reasonable explanation of what he meant by the word "God" and that it was therefore as meaningless to assert a belief as to assert a disbelief in God.

Though this, in a general way, has remained my position ever since, I have always avoided unnecessarily to offend other people holding religious belief by displaying my lack of such belief or even stating my lack of belief, if I was not challenged. On the other hand, my position vis-à-vis the different Christian churches was somewhat ambivalent. I felt that if somebody really wanted religion, he had better stick to what seemed to me the "true article," that is, Roman Catholicism. Protestantism always appeared to me a step in the process of emancipation from a superstition—a step which, once taken, must lead to complete unbelief. Yet its apparent reasonableness might keep a person within the fold of Christianity who could not accept all of the doctrines of Catholicism. In other words, I felt that only the two extremes were tolerably stable positions; but since I had found my resting place in one of these extreme positions, I did not particularly worry, but I may often have seemed inconsistent by *intellectually* sympathizing more with Protestantism yet admitting that, if one must have a religion, Catholicism seemed to me more consistent.

Q_1: Doesn't your thinking in terms of a moral structure—the concept of 'just conduct'—at least get at some very fundamental part of religious precepts?

HAYEK: I think it does go to the question which people try to answer by religion: that there are in the surrounding world a great many orderly phenomena which we cannot understand and which we have to accept. In a way, I've recently discovered that the polytheistic religions of Buddhism appeal rather more to me than the monotheistic religions of the West. If they confine themselves, as some Buddhists do, to a profound respect for the existence of other orderly structures in the world, which they admit they cannot fully understand and interpret, I think it's an admirable attitude.

So far as I do feel hostile to religion, it's against monotheistic religions, because they are so frightfully intolerant. All monotheistic religions are intolerant and try to enforce their particular creed. I've just been looking a little into the Japanese position, where you don't even have to belong to one religion. Almost every Japanese is Shintoist in one respect and Buddhist in the other, and this is recognized as reconcilable. Every Japanese is born, married, and buried as a Shintoist, but all his beliefs are Buddhist. I think that's an admirable state of affairs.

I passed through a variety of schools, changing the *Volkschule* [elementary school] once because of a move and *Gymnasium* twice because I ran into difficulties with my teachers, who were irritated by the combination of obvious ability and laziness and lack of interest I showed. Except for biology, few of the school subjects interested me, and I consistently neglected my homework, counting on picking up enough during lessons to scrape through. Normally I succeeded in swotting up enough at the end of the year, when doubtful candidates were allowed a critical test called a *Forsetzungsprüfung*. But once, in the fourth year, when I had failed in all three critical subjects—Latin, Greek, and mathematics—even this opportunity was denied to me, and I had to repeat the form. One good effect of this was that I became really familiar with Homer, and got to know and like Homeric Greek, for in that particular year they were reading Homer in the Greek classes. In 1916, when my form was to get again the leading master with whom I ran foul in 1913, I changed once more to another *Gymnasium*, where I remained, however, little more than five months before going into the army.

My first scientific interest was, following my father, in botany. He had early interested me in the collection of natural specimens of various sorts—minerals, insects, and flowers—and as he owned a remarkably large herbarium and for many years edited a "flora Exicata" [the organized supply and exchange of rare specimens of pressed plants], I had much opportunity to help him, first as a collector and later as photographer—the hobby which from about age thirteen to sixteen engaged much of my spare time. I also started my own herbarium and even began a monograph on *Orchis condigera*, an effort from which I was discouraged mainly by my persistent failure to find a live specimen of this rare species (or, probably, only a variety). Systematic botany with its puzzle of the existence of clearly defined classes proved a useful education. But my interest gradually shifted from botany to paleontology and the theory of evolution. I must have been about sixteen when I began to find man more interesting, and for a time played with the idea of becoming a psychiatrist. Also public life and certain aspects of social organization—such as education, the press, political parties—began to interest me, not so much as subjects for systematic study but from a desire to comprehend the world in which I was living.

I sometimes regret that I was too young when my father, recognizing my intellectual dissatisfaction with the taxonomic aspects of biology and my longing for theory, put the two heavy volumes of Weismann's *Vorträge über Deszendenztheorie* in my hands. They were still entirely beyond my comprehension and my power of persistent work. I believe that if I had returned to them a few years later, at the time when external circumstances drew my interests to social phenomena, I would have become a biologist. The subject has retained for me an unceasing fascination, and work in that field would have satisfied my inclination for patient search for significant facts, an inclination which by the nature of the subject is permanently frustrated in economic theory and had to find its outlets in occasional dabbling in biographical, genealogical, and similar amusements.

Q6: Was your training in biology primarily in the *Gymnasium*?

HAYEK: No, not what I learned at school, but at home. Most of the influence comes from my father, and the family tradition, collecting everything. I started keeping my own herbarium and—my first attempt at a piece of scientific work—began to do a study of a supposed species of orchid. It was a question of whether it was a separate species or only a variety. Thus I was introduced into taxonomy;

then Father was perceptive enough to see that my mind was more theoretical than it was in taxonomy. He put into my hands two volumes on the theory of evolution, just a year too early. If he had put Weismann and DeVries into my hands a year later, I would probably have stuck with biology. But I got dissatisfied with the taxonomic work and gradually withdrew.

The great disturbances of war got me more interested in economics. While I was at the university, I was still in doubt between economics and psychology. Law and economics gave one a chance of an occupation. After the death of Stöhr, there wasn't even anyone teaching psychology. What psychology I knew, I got myself from books. There was no opportunity for learning anything else.

Although at school commonly regarded as intelligent but lazy and always a voracious reader, I do not think I was then of the "intellectual" type, and my ambition was directed more to becoming efficient in handling the practical details of life than in scholarship as such. Whether it was photography or skiing, the use of books or various kinds of collecting, I used my intelligence largely to acquire techniques or to master the theoretical foundations of practical activities rather than intellectual problems as such which occupied me. I had a strong desire to equip myself for the practical tasks of life, to learn how to organize things and particularly my own affairs, in short, to be efficient. For some time my model was the fire-brigade horse—who was stabled in the firehouse with his harness hanging above him, ready at the shortest notice without loss of time—and trying to simplify and mechanize routines as much as possible.

During my sixteenth and seventeenth years or thereabouts, I developed a great interest in the drama, and this must have been the first interest which I pursued systematically for some time and where I showed real initiative. I not only became a very frequent visitor to the *Burgtheater* and informed myself about its history but I began to read widely, including translations of most of the Spanish and French dramatists of the seventeenth and eighteenth centuries as well as of the ancient Greek dramas. (The German "classics" and the German versions of the main plays of Shakespeare I had come to know early, partly from my father reading them aloud to us in the evening.) By about 1916

I must have had quite an extensive acquaintance with dramatic literature, including such relatively modern authors as Ibsen and Björnson, and less well known figures such as Hebbel (whose complete works in a currently published edition was one of my first major book purchases). I even started to write tragedies myself, on rather violent and more or less erotic historical themes (Andromache, Rosamund, etc.), but I never finished a play, though I usually was working up towards some rather effective concluding scenes I had thought out.

Q$_6$: Do you remember any of the plots?

HAYEK: There is one which occupied me most for quite a long time. It was a play about Andromache. With all the implications; very obscure, and only half understood. But ending in a magnificent scene—which indeed would be theatrically very effective—Andromache is the slave of Achilles's son, wandering from the castle out onto the sea, onto a rock extending out into the sea, and the sun rises and she runs up to the sun: "It's you, it's you, my Hector." And she falls into the sea.

I joined a field artillery regiment at Vienna in March 1917, and after a little over seven months' training was sent as a sergeant-major-officer-cadet (if I can thus translate the even longer title) to the Italian front where I served for a little over a year. I missed my battery near Gorizia on the Isonzo, where it had just left in pursuit of the Italians after the battle of Caporetto, and caught up with it a few days later, and spent nearly all the year in position in the left bank of the Piave River. The most exciting moments were one abortive offensive in June 1918, the collapse of the Austro-Hungarian army in October 1918, and the two waves of retreat. Most of the later part of the period we were more concerned with hunger, disease, and the rumors of a mutiny of the Czechs than with serious fighting. Like most of my comrades, I managed to contract an infection of malaria, which broke out only during the retreat, so that I finally returned to Vienna towards the middle of November 1918 in a somewhat weakened state (to which a severe attack of flu earlier in the summer had contributed its part).

The first time I really proved to myself (what I seem never to have seriously doubted) that if I really wanted I could, without much effort, do as well as the best of my fellows was in the officers' school in the army. It gave me then considerable pleasure that even on such purely technological details as, say, the variable recoil mechanism of a howitzer, I was never as much at home as any of my more mechanically minded contemporaries; and that in spite of a lack of any special natural aptitudes, and even in spite of a certain clumsiness, which prevented me from excelling as horseman or draftsman as some of my colleagues did, I emerged among the five or six heading the list of some seventy or eighty cadets.

In a way of course I was even then somewhat more academic, less familiar with the everyday world (and particularly with women) and more at home with books than most of my contemporaries. But this (except for my innocence on some very worldly matters) was still much less true of me than of the one or two really intellectual and highly sophisticated among that group. Compared with these much more mature young soldiers, I was then and for some years to come still a child.

Q_2: I seem to recall a story I once heard you tell. You presided over the retreat of some troops. You were a lieutenant and ran into quite an interesting—

HAYEK: It wasn't very interesting. On the retreat from the Piave [River], we were first pursued by the Italians. Since I was telephone officer of my regiment—which meant that I knew all the very few German-speaking men, who were the only reliable men in these conditions—I was asked to take a little detachment for the artillery regiment, first as a rear guard against the Italians following us and then as an advance guard as we were passing the Yugoslav part, where there were irregular Yugoslav cadres who were trying to stop us and get our guns. On that occasion, after having fought for a year without ever having to do a thing like that, I had to attack a firing machine gun. In the night, by the time I had got to the machine gun, they had gone. But it was an unpleasant experience.

The interest in history and public affairs, completely lacking in me as a boy, was awakened mainly through contact with a slightly older friend, Walter Magg, the only close childhood friend whom I had. He was two years older than I and exceptionally gifted, very musical (unlike myself), and with a broad literary education and a facility for writing which at that time was wholly beyond me. He was mature for his age, and this for a time drew us apart, but I caught up, and between 1915 and 1917 he had a great influence on the development of my interests. He joined the army some time ahead of me and died from a disease contracted on active service in Laibach [Ljubliana] in October 1917 a few days after I had passed through the place on the way to join my battery without being able to see him.

The beginning of my definite interest in economics I can clearly date back to a logic lesson in the seventh form of the *Gymnasium*, late in 1916, when the master explained to us the threefold Aristotelian division of ethics into morals, politics, and economics—which seemed to me perfectly to cover the field in which I was interested. My father was rather alarmed when I suddenly declared that I intended to study "ethics," and a few days later, in order to convince me what nonsense ethics was, presented me with four works of the philosopher Ludwig Feuerbach which he had picked up in a secondhand bookshop. I must confess that I found this particular philosopher merely a bore and only much later gained access to serious philosophy. Nor did I at that time really find out what economics was about. My reading then was mainly ephemeral pamphlets of contemporary politics, mostly of a socialist or semi-socialist character, from Karl Renner to Walter Rathenau, from the latter of whom I derived most of my first economics ideas. (In the autumn of 1917, during the short leave from the army that I took in order to obtain my *matura*, I actually got into trouble in the *Gymnasium* when I was found reading a socialist pamphlet during the divinity lesson.) It was only sometime in 1917 or 1918, during a quiet period on the field on the Piave, that one of the slightly senior officers in my battery gave me the first systematic books on economics, and I still marvel that the particular books did not give me a permanent distaste for the subject. But I seriously waded through these two volumes (by Gruntzl and Jentsch), which were as poor specimens of economics as can be imagined.

Q₂: Since you came from a family of natural scientists, how did you get interested in the social sciences?

HAYEK: I think the decisive influence was really World War I, particularly the experience of serving in a multinational army, the Austro-Hungarian army. That's when I saw, more or less, the great empire collapse over the nationalist problem. I served in a battle in which eleven different languages were spoken. It's bound to draw your attention to the problems of political organization.

It was during the war service in Italy that I more or less decided to do economics. But I really got hooked when I found [Carl] Menger's *Grundsätze* such a fascinating book, so satisfying. Even then, you see, I came back to study law in order to be able to do economics, but I was about equally interested in economics and psychology. I finally had to choose between the things I was interested in. Economics at least had a formal legitimation by a degree, while in psychology you had nothing. And since there was no opportunity of a job, I decided for economics.

My plans had been, in part for immediate practical reasons, a career which, after a simultaneous study of law at the university and languages and international problems at the *Konsularakademie* [a special school for future diplomats], would lead to the diplomatic service and perhaps through it later to an academic or political position. But with the collapse of Austria-Hungary, the *Konsularakademie* disappeared, and the diplomatic part of this scheme lost much of its attraction. The law remained as a study which would combine economics with the preparation for either advocacy (the "bar") or, as I thought more likely, the civil service.

Though I returned in November 1918 rather late for the semester and with a severe infection of malaria, I plunged at once with what now seems to me an astounding energy both into several branches of study and, at least in the following spring, a very active social life. I must for weeks have worked hard all day and danced most evenings, though light restrictions in that winter of coal shortage prevented the evenings from becoming too long.

The two chief subjects of discussion among students of the University of Vienna in the years immediately after the war were

Marxism and psychoanalysis, as they were to become much later
in the West. I made a conscientious effort to study both the
doctrines but found them the more unsatisfactory the more I
studied them. It seemed to me then and has so appeared ever
since that their doctrines were thoroughly unscientific because
they so defined their terms that their statements were necessarily true and unrefutable, and therefore said nothing about the
world. It was in the struggle with these views that I developed
views on the philosophy of science rather similar to, but of
course much less clearly formulated than, those which Karl Popper formed from much the same experiences; and it was only
natural that I read his views when he published *The Logic of
Scientific Discovery* in 1935, some years before I made his acquaintance.

Q_6: Vienna was almost a capital of intellectual ferment from what I
can see, from 1880 or 1890, probably through the 1930s. Is that
how you perceive it in retrospect?

HAYEK: You can date it exactly. The great reform in 1867; till then
the University of Vienna was nothing, nothing. Eighteen hundred
sixty-seven it begins to grow; at the end of the century it reached a
high point. It had its highest level in the 1890s and up to 1914. It revived once more after the war, through the 1920s, and almost at the
beginning of the 1930s it dies, not only in economics, all of it.

*　*　*

Q_4: When I look at this period, a lot of people—this is true also before the war and for those who were young men after the war—
often describe themselves as positivists or antipositivists, and I have
difficulty in knowing what positivism actually meant at that time.

HAYEK: It was almost entirely the influence of Ernst Mach, the physicist, and his disciples. He was the most influential figure philosophi-
cally. At that time, apart from what I had been reading before I
joined the army, I think my introduction to what I now almost hesitate to call philosophy—scientific method, I think, is a better description—was through Machian philosophy. It was very good on the
history of science generally, and it dominated discussion in Vienna.
Joseph Schumpeter had fully fallen for Mach, and while I was still at
the university, this very interesting figure, Moritz Schlick, became

one of the professors of philosophy. It was the beginning of the Vienna circle, of which I was, of course, never a member, but whose members were in close contact with us. There was one man [Felix Kaufmann] who was supposedly a member of our particular circle, the *Geistkreis*, and also the Schlick circle, the Vienna circle proper, and so we were currently informed of what was happening there.

What dissuaded me is that the social scientists, the science specialists in the tradition of Otto Neurath, just were so extreme and so naive on economics; it was actually through them that I became aware that positivism was just misleading in the social sciences. I owe it to Neurath's extreme position that I recognized it wouldn't do. And it took me a long time, really, to emancipate myself from it. It was only after I had left Vienna, in London, that I began to think systematically on problems of methodology in the social sciences, and I began to recognize that positivism in that field was definitely misleading.

In a discussion I had on a visit to Vienna from London with my friend Haberler, I explained to him that I had come to the conclusion that all this Machian positivism was no good for our purposes. Then he countered, "Oh, there's a very good new book that came out in the circle of Vienna positivists by a man called Karl Popper on the logic of scientific research." So I became one of the early readers. It had just come out a few weeks before. I found that Haberler had been rather mistaken by the setting in which the book had appeared. While it came formally out of that circle, it was really an attack on that system. And to me it was so satisfactory because it confirmed this certain view I had already formed due to an experience very similar to Karl Popper's. Karl Popper is four or five years my junior, so we did not belong to the same academic generation. But our environment in which we formed our ideas was very much the same. It was very largely dominated by discussion, on the one hand, with Marxists and, on the other hand, with Freudians.

Both these groups had one very irritating attribute: They insisted that their theories were, in principle, irrefutable. I remember particularly one occasion when I suddenly began to see how ridiculous it all was when I was arguing with Freudians, and they explained, "Oh, well, this is due to the death instinct." And I said, "But this can't be due to the death instinct." "Oh, then this is due to the life instinct." Naturally, if you have these two alternatives available to explain something, there's no way of checking whether the theory is true or not. And that led me, already, to the understanding of what became Popper's main systematic point: that the test of empirical science was that it could be refuted, and that any system which claimed that it was irrefutable was by definition not scientific. I was not a trained philosopher; I didn't elaborate this. It was sufficient for me to have recognized this, but when I found this thing explicitly argued and justified in Popper, I just accepted the Popperian philosophy for spelling out what I had always felt.

Ever since, I have been moving with Popper. We became ultimately very close friends, although we had not known each other in Vienna. To a very large extent I have agreed with him, although not always immediately. Popper has had his own interesting developments, but on the whole I agree with him more than with anybody else on philosophical matters.

* * *

Q$_6$: To what extent was there a feeling of free thought in Vienna? Could you make a comparison to the freedom of thought and the flourishing of the music through Vienna, of Mozart, and Beethoven, and Wagner, and all of these people—is there any comparison to be made there?

HAYEK: I don't think it was so much a feeling of freedom. I'd say in the university, the decisive point was simply that you were not expected to confine yourself to your own subject. I must have spent as much time in lectures on other fields, with other people, as I did in economics. Nominally I was studying law, but still it left me time, or I took time. I spent my day at the university from morning till evening, but shifting from subject to subject, readily hearing lectures about art history or ancient Greek plays or something else. Curiously enough, it so happens that psychology had died out by natural death during the wartime. There had been during the war two eminent psychologists who had fought and died, there was still one [Adolf Stöhr] dying painfully, still giving daily lectures, but you could see this had been a brilliant man for whom now the effort was to get a word out—but he was sufficiently interesting to attract me. And so it was for others.

It all happened at a time when the university was overflooded by veterans who were coming from the war. The number of students was probably three times normal, of whom nine-tenths wanted to get their degree as rapidly as possible. Yet some of us managed in an equally short period not only to get, as I did, a first-class degree in law, but to study half a dozen other subjects. The university welcomed this. There never was any test.

I also attended any number of other lectures where I had no right at all. I was going around all through the university, testing out people. I would try people like the famous Kammerer—you probably remember the name, Koestler wrote a book about him. Here was a man who believed he could prove the inheritance of acquired characteristics, and became for a moment very famous. There were some very original figures. Also at the university there were, outside what you could call the professional staff, these *Privatdozenten* who were just licensed to lecture, with their own ideas, who didn't take part in the organized scheme at all, but who came in in an effort to persuade the students of their ideas. So the variety we had in the 1920s at the University of Vienna was unlimited.

Q6: It sounds very much like the University of Berlin in Marx's day. The same coffeehouse atmosphere, the brilliant young men coming in of all persuasions. Of course in their case I guess Hegel would have been the overriding influence, in the way Mach was in your day.

HAYEK: Probably was. I mean the contrast—another subject—between the University of Vienna as I knew it and the present is such that I avoid going to Vienna. In every other respect, Vienna is beautifully revived. It's nice that it has become economically prosperous. But what I remember was desperately poor, with this great intellectual excitement about. The main people who taught were absolutely first-class people. Every lecturer, nearly every one, was intelligent and perhaps had contributed. They had to be, in order to have any students. If someone was bad, he wouldn't have any students.

Q6: I have never heard of a university since medieval times where that was true. You mean to say that the lectures really counted for something. The students actually went to lectures because they were good lectures. I'm thinking of people like you who went here and there and everywhere. Was that common?

HAYEK: There was a small group of us who did it, a very small group. But I was by no means alone. I had friends with whom I talked who would have tried something else, and who would tell me, it's worth going to this and that, because they experimented in the same way I did.

Q_6: Let me get back to the original question. Was there a relationship between what was going on in Vienna, and the openness—if it was openness, I gather that it must have been—and what was going on at the university, which sounds like another equally important experiment in the sharing of ideas.

HAYEK: The university was a world to itself. There were at the university, at least in the law faculty, often very violent political discussions, involving the organized socialists and communists. In fact, even I, although I've never since belonged to a political party, was along with my friends organizing a German Democratic party when I was a student in 1918–21, in order to have a middle group between the Catholics on one side and the socialists and communists on the other side.

In spite of this, I did complete my law studies in a year short of the official time, because I had veterans' credits, which meant that I was allowed to in a shorter period, and I managed to do it. In spite of a complication—I came back from war with a fairly severe case of malaria. I was not in the best of health, but having to spend every other evening at home with a high temperature didn't very much interfere with the rest of it.

I have fairly detailed information of both what lectures I attended and what I read during this period so far as economics is concerned. At the time I started my studies at the University of Vienna, the law faculty was very brilliant, but economics for the moment was almost unrepresented. Among the lawyers there were some great scholars, like Wlassak in Roman law and Stooss (criminal law); and a few brilliant lecturers like Bernatzik (who died halfway through an encyclopedic introduction to the political sciences to which I went during my first year); and exceptional teachers like Pisko (commercial law) and Loeffler (criminal law).

After some months, Friedrich von Wieser, who had been minister of commerce in the last government of the Austrian Empire, was reappointed to the chair in economics, although my closer contacts with him occurred only in my last year at the university and the year immediately following my getting the degree. At the time, a stronger though short-lived influence came from a younger man, Othmar Spann, appointed to the second chair in political economy about the same time, and at first most successful in attracting the students by his enthusiasm, unconventionality, and interest in their individual activities.

I don't think I learnt much from Spann, certainly not in that seminar on methodology, the first seminar I ever attended, which was much above my head but also, I believe, unintelligible to most of the other participants. But he did make me read a few good books, particularly Carl Menger's, of which he did not then so violently disapprove as he did later, and from his *Fundament der Volkswirtschaftslehre* I got a few helpful ideas about the significance of the logic of the means-ends structure in economics theory. We did not get on together long, and after a short period in which I had been regarded as one of his favorites, he in effect turned me out of his seminar by telling me that by my constant carping criticism I confused the younger members.

Q6: My first question was on Menger. He did not want to publish, and yet he had enormous impact on the ideas. What was the character of Menger as a teacher or as a personality which made those ideas carry forth even though he wrote so little?

HAYEK: That's a question which I've often asked myself. I hardly knew Menger. I've seen him a single time, when he was about eighty, long retired, marching in an academic procession; and the comic part of this story is, when later I wrote a biographical essay on him, editing his works, there is one single sentence which is based on my own experience and that is the only one which is wrong. Because he made a very impressive figure, I described him as a tall man, and afterwards everyone told me I was wrong, he was quite medium-sized. He was such an impressive figure that after seeing him I described him as a tall man!

Now, at his seminar, when he retired, there was a small group of

very intelligent people—former students who were already occupying important positions—who had regular meetings in a coffeehouse: a "Menger circle." That was dominant the very last third of
the last century, and since Menger retired in 1903, very little was
left at the beginning of the century. During World War I, the most
powerful personal figure among his students, Böhm-Bawerk, also
died, and so did the great textbook expositor Philippovich. Indeed
even a third man, who later became my teacher, Friedrich von
Wieser, had temporarily left the university. So when I came back
from the war in 1918, there was not a single one of three great
teachers still teaching. In fact, economics was in the charge—
temporarily and rather comically—of an economic historian who
was a socialist and became later the founder of the famous Marxist-
Freudian Frankfurt Institute of Social Research. But Wieser came
back.

Q_6: Who was that?

HAYEK: Karl Grünberg was his name. Later people at the Frankfurt Institute were the representative figures of Marx-Freud traditions in the
nineteenth century. He himself was an economic historian inclined
in that direction, the sort of scholarly head for something which became a very political institution. But wholly uninteresting to us.
Then there was Wieser, who came back, and became my teacher.

Q_6: Did students meet with the senior professor over coffee?

HAYEK: In one particular instance that I knew very well, the early
morning lecture, the students would come if they wanted to consult
the professor. For the students, the coffee shop across the street, although it was very modest, seemed too luxurious a place to go to,
while the Vienna coffeehouse, where in fact you could spend a day
paying for a single cup of coffee, was very attractive for intellectuals
of a slightly higher level than the average student, the student coffee
being still cheaper in the university. But the professor who after his
lecture retired to his cup of coffee would receive others.

I suspect, but I do not know, that like the younger men I knew,
Menger also would have met his people at the Kaffee Landmann,
but in Menger's case the main importance was that it was not
students, but ex-students, who met regularly in a kind of circle
discussing current politics. While Menger never became active in
current Austrian politics, as an influence behind the scene and the

intellectual heart of nineteenth-century liberals, he became very, very important. And the high civil servants who would have been his students in the 1870s would in the 1890s and the beginning of the century regularly come once a week for a conversation with Menger.

Q₆: What about Böhm-Bawerk's seminar? Let's talk about that.

HAYEK: That was quite a different affair. That was the center of the academic development. Böhm-Bawerk and Wieser, as you will see from this, were wholly different characters. It's very curious, they were exact contemporaries, schoolfellows, university colleagues, brothers-in-law, working on the same subject, going together to German university, but of a wholly different scientific attitude. I've once written an essay with the title "Two Types of Mind," which was partly modelled on this contrast. Böhm-Bawerk was the absolute master of his subject, he knew the answer to everything; anything which had been said before, he knew, a clear conception of it all.

Q₆: And Wieser was the puzzler.

HAYEK: With a tendency to simplify, in order to avoid certain difficulties. Wieser was a slow, thoughtful person, to whom nothing was simple, it was all frightfully difficult, who hated discussing anything because he had to give a quick answer. He wanted to think above everything else.

Q₆: We hear very little of Wieser's students; we hear mostly of Böhm-Bawerk's students. Is there a reason for that?

HAYEK: Yes; the seminars are wholly different affairs. Böhm-Bawerk's seminars were highly exciting. He had, apart from the main original thinkers of his own school, a good many of the socialists of the time, people like Otto Bauer, with violent discussions going on. What was discussed in Böhm-Bawerk's seminar was discussed all over the university. Wieser's seminar would be quiet, with one neat theoretical problem—a carefully prepared paper, which they would pick to pieces, but very far away from any topical issue of any kind. The Böhm-Bawerk seminar ended before World War I; he died in 1914 or 1915. I've only known the Wieser seminar. It was interesting from a theoretical view, but nothing to get excited about.

Q₆: Were you in both?

HAYEK: When Böhm-Bawerk died, I was sixteen. I knew Böhm-Bawerk only by chance, because he happened to be a friend of my grandfather, my maternal grandfather, and he was at the same time professor at Innsbruck in the 1880s. Actually, it may also amuse you, they used to climb mountains together, and it was still possible in the 1880s to do some first ascents together to some of the peaks. Before my grandfather died, I used to meet Böhm-Bawerk in his house, before I knew what the word "economics" meant. He was just a close friend of my parents and grandparents. Later I used to meet his widow, a maternal friend of my mother; my mother called his widow "aunt," because of the years they were together in Salzburg.

* * *

Q₅: What was the greatest influence you experienced from the Austrian economists?

HAYEK: I was a direct student of Wieser, and he originally had the greatest influence on me. I only met [Ludwig von] Mises really after I had taken my degree. But I now realize—I wouldn't have known it at the time—that the decisive influence was just reading Menger's *Grundsätze*. I probably derived more from not only the *Grundsätze* but also the *Methodenbuch,* not for what it says on methodology but for what it says on general sociology. This conception of the spontaneous generation of institutions is worked out more beautifully there than in any other book I know.

It is difficult to overestimate how much I owe to the fact that, almost from the beginning of my university career, I became connected with a group of contemporaries who belonged to the best type of the Jewish intelligentsia of Vienna and who proved to be far ahead of me in literary education and general precociousness. For the first time, a certain ambition to rival my colleagues in their achievement began to have some influence on my work, and since at that time my serious interests were probably more widely spread than theirs, I managed—while keeping pace with them in my legal and economics studies and to get accepted as one of the half-dozen or so outstanding members of the various seminars—to do a good deal more work than even they did. That I finally not only made up for the year I had lost at school but even beat my closest associates by a few weeks in getting my doctor's degree in law was one of the minor triumphs which gave me the confidence that I could achieve what I seriously wanted to achieve.

Perhaps more so than during my actual university years, I profited from that group in the following period when, at the suggestion of one of them, J. Herbert von Fürth—with whom I had become more intimately connected than with any of the rest—we continued to meet in fortnightly discussion groups. The other members were almost all lawyers with strong philosophic, historical, and literary interests. Nearly all of them are now in America: Max Mintz, Erik Vögelin, Alfred Schutz, Walter Fröhlich, Felix Kaufmann, and, of those who joined later, Gottfried Haberler, Oskar Morgenstern, Fritz Machlup, and Friedrich Engel-Janosi. In part it was the same circle who also met in Mises's *Privatseminar*, when I believe I was for the first time admitted—another important source of stimulation.

Not the least gain which I owed to these Jewish or partly Jewish friends of that period is that they were much more internationally minded than my own circle, that at least what went on in the intellectual world of France and England was to them nearly as familiar as what happened in the German-speaking world. I found names which were quite new to me, like Bertrand Russell or H. G. Wells, Proust or Croce, the names of men with whose ideas one had to be familiar to take part in ordinary conversation. My friends of course belonged mostly to that progressive intelligentsia with more or less strong socialist leanings but a general background of nineteenth-century liberalism. Ambitious and able, they had practically without exception brought from the *Gymnasium* a much better retained stock of general knowledge than I had, and in addition had a command of foreign languages and at least a superficial knowledge of the arts and of literature which I could only envy. And where I learnt perhaps most from them was in the fact that genuine devotion to things of the spirit need not mean being impractical in the art of getting on in life, that a special gift in one field is no excuse for not learning how best to utilize it, and that ignorance of opportunities is as much a result of a particular kind of laziness or a prejudiced disdain for a necessary task as any other lack of capacity to make oneself useful. Though generally these men came from homes which were or had been wealthier than mine, and though no doubt they clung closely together in the struggle against the prejudice they met, they had even then in this prejudice to overcome an obstacle much greater than an equally able Christian of good family, to whom every door was open in Vienna.

Q_6: Was it anti-Semitism which kept Mises from a professorship?

HAYEK: Now please be discreet about this point, because it raises very touchy problems, but it is commonly believed, and Mises himself asserted it, that he was never given a professorship because of anti-Semitism. Actually I suspect it is not as simple as this, because half the law faculty consisted of Jews, and the problem why Mises didn't get a professorship is a very peculiar one; and my answer to this, which I don't think has ever been stated, but I will tell you this, in order for a Jew to get a professorship he had to have the support of his Jewish fellows. Any other Jews who were sufficiently eminent must be supported, because only appointed Jews could get a professorship. But the Jews who were teaching were all socialists, and Mises was an anti-socialist, so he could not get the support of his own fellows. So the reason why he did not get a professorship was not really anti-Semitism, but [that] he wasn't liked by his Jewish colleagues. This is a very comic story, which I tell you with hesitation, because it's the sort of thing you cannot prove. I'm quite certain it's correct.

But the Vienna of the 1920s and 1930s is not intelligible without the Jewish problem. Which was not a problem simply of Christians and Jews but a very large middle group in between the two, partly of baptized Jews, partly of Christians who had made friends with the Jews; and there was close contact between the purely Christian group and the mixed group, and again between the mixed group and the Jewish group, but not between the two extremes. I became very much aware of this quite recently, when I was asked whom of the great figures of Vienna I'd known at the time. For instance, Schrödinger, yes, of course; Wittgenstein, yes, of course; and so on. Then he came to Freud, and I couldn't possibly have known Freud. Why? Because he belonged to the really Jewish group, and that was beyond my range of acquaintances. I had a great many very close acquaintances in the mixed group, I constantly moved in it, but to have met somebody in the purely Jewish group was so unlikely that being told that because I was a Viennese, I ought to have known Freud, seemed to me absurd.

Q₆: Was not Freud a *Privatdozent* for many years himself? Did he ever take a university position?

HAYEK: Never. Both Mises and Freud had the title "professor," but it was purely a title. They were *Privatdozenten,* had a license to teach, and they were called "professor," but never received a penny from the university.

Q₆: Can you tell us something of your relationship with your cousin Ludwig Wittgenstein?

HAYEK: I can't say I knew him well, but of course I knew him over a much longer period than anybody now alive [in 1983]. My first recollection goes back to a day on furlough and leave of absence from the front, where on the railway station in Bad Ischl [Austria], two young ensigns in the artillery in uniform looked at each other and said, "You have a fairly familiar face." Then we asked each other, "Aren't you a Wittgenstein?" and "Aren't you a Hayek?" I now know that at this moment returning to the front, he must have had the manuscript of the *Tractatus* in his rucksack. But I didn't know it at the time. But many of the mental characteristics of the man were already present, as I gathered in this night journey from Bad Ischl to Innsbruck, where the occasion was his contempt for the noisy crowd of returning young officers, half-drunk; a certain contempt for the world.

Then I didn't see him for a long time, but I heard a lot about it because his oldest sister was a close friend of my mother's. They were second cousins, and she came frequently to our house. There were little rumors constant about this crazy young man, but she strongly defended Wittgenstein, and that's how I heard about him.

But I came to know him much later in Cambridge. I met him there before the war; I saw him in the later part of the war when he returned, but we never really did talk philosophy. I have a strong impression of the kind of personality. The last discussion I had with him was a discussion on politics. We were both returning from Vienna, but I had broken the journey in Basle and stepped into a sleeping car at midnight in Basle, and it turned out that my companion in the sleeping car was Wittgenstein. And all during the first half of the following morning we were—as soon as he had finished his detective story—first talking about Vienna and the Russians in Vienna, and this led to talk about philosophy and ethical problems; he was bitterly disappointed about what he had seen of the Russians then. And just when it became interesting, we arrived at the port for the ferry. And although he said, "We must continue this," he apparently regretted having gone out of himself, because on the ship he was not to be found, and I never saw him again.

Wittgenstein was three-quarters Jewish. But the family was completely established in Vienna society, as in general you know. The Jewish problem in Vienna became acute only as a result of emigration from Poland. There was an old, established Jewish population in Vienna, partly of local origin, partly of Hungarian or Bohemian origin, who were fully accepted and recognized. The violent anti-Semitism occurred when very primitive, poor Polish Jews immigrated, already before the war and partly in flight from the Russians during the war. Vienna became filled with a type of Jew which hadn't been known before, with cap on and long beards, which we hadn't even seen before. And it was against them that anti-Semitism developed.

Q_6: Was that the 1920s or 1930s?

HAYEK: It was still during the Great War they immigrated; it developed during the 1920s and 1930s, but the immigration occurred during the first Great War.

Q_6: So you regarded yourself as this mixed group—

HAYEK: Not my family, my family is on the purely Christian group; but in the university context I entered into the mixed group. And there were several things which I must confess I resented among our Jewish friends. The worst was that I was not allowed to speak about Jewish things; they did that all the time. Even the theme of "Has he a Jewish accent?" was constantly discussed among them; if I would have said a word about it, it would have been bitterly resented.

In Vienna there was a certain amount of speculation in the Jewish community [about whether my family was Jewish]. One of the things that amused me: My younger brother Heinz, who in every other respect had a face that could be much less Jewish than mine, actually had dark hair, black hair; and it so happened that in one of the summers that I spent in the Schwarzwalds' summer home, I happened to overhear a conversation among the Jewish circle, when my brother arrived, to the effect that he looks Jewish.

My own curiosity about this led me to spend a great deal of time researching my ancestors. I have full information for five generations in all possible directions. And since they all happened to be first-born children, there's more certainty that they derived from their parents; so as far back as I can possibly trace it, I evidently had no Jewish ancestors whatever.

I was of course supposed to study law, and economics constituted merely one subject in one of the three major exams for the final (doctor's) examination. Yet though I not only passed most of the exams with distinction but also succeeded (taking advantage of a special concession to returned soldiers) to take the degree after three years (in November 1921) instead of the usual four, my main interests were long divided between psychology and economics, and later chiefly to economics.

I will, however, first say a little about my brief but intense concern with the problems of physiological psychology, which took up a considerable part of my energies in 1919 and 1920. It had been caused mainly by my interest in the writings of Ernst Mach, then much in vogue among the generation just ahead of me. It was in reading his philosophical writings that I conceived the idea which I vainly tried to explain in a brief paper in 1920 and finally published thirty-two years later in *The Sensory Order*. I had then to acquire my knowledge of psychology practically on my own, since the only man on the faculty who was at all interested in this kind of problem—the philosopher Adolf Stöhr (a rather interesting man)—was already mortally ill and difficult of access. Both he and the German philosopher Alois Riehl—by whose work I had been greatly impressed and to whom I sent an early draft of my essay—gave me just enough encouragement to make me persevere in my efforts. In September 1920, when I had to start systematic work for the main law examination, I put the draft of that essay away—I thought at the time, for a short while; however, I did not concern myself again seriously with these problems until about 1946.

Strictly speaking I devoted only the one academic year (1920–21) to an intense study of modern law, and though this has left some impression on my mind, what legal knowledge I have retained is much more due to the three-semester course on the history of law, and particularly Roman law, than to this year of cramming for the examination. As soon as I had passed the exams, I turned to economics, to which I devoted what spare time the job I had taken even before the last examination left me.

A decisive step in my introduction to economic theory, perhaps the occasion which made me see what it was all about, was when, some time during my first year of the university, somebody introduced me to a group of single-taxers [*Bodenreformers*]—the German version of the Henry George school, led by one Damaschke)—and I was persuaded to read to them a paper on the Ricardian theory of rent. The latter at once fascinated me, while my enthusiasm for the single-tax proposal rapidly ended. I do not remember what flaws in it I found then, because it seems to me to the present day the theoretically most defensible of all socialist proposals and impractical only because of the de facto impossibility of distinguishing between the original and permanent powers of the soil and the different kinds of improvements.

During my three years at the university, I had (in addition to a few days in Munich) two opportunities to visit foreign countries: a visit of about six to eight weeks to Zurich in the winter of 1919–20 (when the University of Vienna was closed because of lack of fuel for heating) and about three or four weeks on an estate in Norway (inland, near Hamar on the lake Mjösen) in late August and September 1920. Both were made possible by invitations from my father's fellow botanists who, as part of the general efforts on behalf of the undernourished German and Austrian children, wanted to help the son of a friend who had recently returned from war and not only needed some feeding up but was also suffering from malaria (from which indeed the visit to Norway seems to have finally cured me).

Intellectually the visit to Zurich was fairly important for me. Apart from the lectures of Fritz Fleiner on canon law (among the most brilliant university lectures I have ever heard), the most lasting effect of my auditing lectures at the University of

Zurich was that a young lecturer talked at some length on a new book (*Erkenntnislehre*) by an author whom his Swiss pronunciation made me believe was called "Moritschlick"—and whose book in consequence for a while I could not trace—but whom after my return to Vienna I soon discovered to be identical with the newly appointed professor of philosophy, Moritz Schlick, who was the first to persuade me that philosophy could make sense, which until then I had found only in the works of Ernst Mach. I worked for a few weeks in the laboratory of the brain anatomist von Monakow, tracing fibre bundles through the different parts of the human brain. Otherwise, Zurich in 1919–20 gave me a first taste in the postwar period of what a "normal" society could be like, Vienna still being in the throes of inflation and semistarvation.

One of the reasons I rather hurried to get my degree was that I had hoped before taking a job to spend an additional year at a German university. Max Weber had taught in Vienna the year I was fighting in Italy, and when I returned the following year, the university was full of talk about that great man. I in fact got a half-promise from my father that after getting my degree at Vienna I might go for a year to Munich. Max Weber, however, died before that moment came, and the later stages of the Austrian inflation would in any case have made it altogether impossible for my father to pay the costs of my studying for a year in Germany. In consequence, after a long summer vacation, in 1921 I started looking for a job, and in October, immediately after I had passed the last examination and even before I had the degree conferred upon me, started, later in October 1921, working at the government office to which Wieser had recommended me and of which Mises was one of the directors. The office, a temporary agency set up to carry out certain financial clauses of the peace treaty, was called the *Abrechnungsamt* [Office of Accounts].

After entering the *Abrechnungsamt*, I continued to register at the university for the degree of *doctor rerum politicarum*, and in the summer of 1922 started work on a thesis on the theory of imputation, for which I got my second degree in February or March 1923, just before I went to America. Though I learnt a great deal in the work and the article on *Zurechnung* [imputation of value] which later emerged from it is a fairly respectable performance, I rather hope that no copies of the thesis have survived. (It existed only in a few typewritten copies, and I am told that the University Library of Vienna, which ought to have the one accessible to the public, cannot trace it.)

My early visit to the United States, from March 1923 to May 1924, was undertaken at my own risk before Rockefeller fellowships and the like became available to Central European students. I had made up my mind that an acquaintance with the States was indispensable for an economist, and the opportunity arose when in the spring of 1922 I met in Vienna Professor Jeremiah W. Jenks of New York University. When I told him of my desire, he said that he was planning to write during the following year a book on Central Europe and, if I made my way to New York, he would employ me for a few months as a research assistant.

Somehow I managed between the end of the inflation in the summer of 1922 and early 1923 to save enough money to pay the single fare to New York and arrived there with scarcely more than $20 in my pocket, only to find that Professor Jenks had left for a vacation and given instructions that he was not to be disturbed. After presenting the letters of introduction which Schumpeter (on whom, as president of the Biederman Bank, which soon after failed, I had called for the purpose) had given me to various economists without their opening an alternative, I started job hunting with steadily declining hopes.

With my very inadequate knowledge of English and at the time of a marked recession of trade, the prospects were slim, and after a fortnight, when my funds were wholly exhausted, I was finally accepted as a dishwasher in a Sixth Avenue restaurant—but I never actually started on it, since an hour before I was to report to work a telephone call came through saying that Professor Jenks had returned and was prepared to employ me. I worked for him for about six months at $100 a month, living on $60 and saving during the period enough to have the return fare to Europe in my pocket. After that, Jenks got me a small studentship at New York University, intended for little more than the tuition fees, but on which I managed to live for another nine months (in a Y.M.C.A.).

Though officially registered at New York University where I started on a Ph.D. thesis under J. D. Magee, I gate-crashed a good deal into lectures at Columbia University, especially the lectures of W. C. Mitchell on the history of economics and the last seminar J. B. Clark ever gave—in which I read the last paper.

During the first six months in New York, I used my spare time, while working for Jenks in the New York Public Library, to turn my Vienna thesis on imputation of value [*Zurechnung*] into an article which Wieser had given me to understand might be used for the *Handwörterbuch der Staatswissenschaften* but which ultimately appeared in Conrad's *Jahrbücher*. On the whole I felt somewhat tired of the subjects which had chiefly occupied me in Vienna during the preceding year or so, such as the theory of subjective value or the problem of economic calculation under socialism, and I was looking for a suitable descriptive subject for which I could use my visit to America. (In the field of pure theory, I found the American universities somewhat disappointing but found much that was wholly new to me in the newly developed techniques for the statistical analysis of economic time series.) I soon began collecting material for a book on the development of the Federal Reserve System that I intended to write after my return to Vienna, but all that came of it was an article in several parts on recent American monetary policy in the *Zeitschrift für Volkswirtschaft* and a lecture on the Federal Reserve System which appeared in the *Österreichische Volkswirt* ["Die Währungspolitik der Vereinigten Staaten seit der Uberwindung der Krise von 1920" and "Das amerikanische Bankwesen seit der Reform von 1914"].

After my work for Jenks was completed and he had got me the scholarship at New York University, I worked for a time for Willard Thorp, collecting the Central European (German, Austrian, and Italian) material for his *Business Annals*, an occupation which taught me much, both as regards the facts of the history of industrial fluctuations and as regards the techniques of utilizing library resources. Thorp and B. H. Beckhart (who

was working on the same table in the economics research room
of the New York Public Library on his book on the discount
policy of the Federal Reserve System) became my most regular
companions, or rather the only people of whom I saw a fair
amount and through whom I made some contacts with other
young economists.

I had hoped to prolong my stay in the States for another year
by means of a Rockefeller fellowship, for which I had been
proposed as the first Austrian candidate by Wieser. But the notification of the award reached New York a few hours after I had
started my return journey to Vienna, which shortage of funds
did not allow me to delay. It caught up with me after my arrival
in Vienna, but I was then unwilling and unable, in view of my
job, to take it up at once, hoping to go instead a few years
later. But before this became possible, I had married and taken
another job which bound me to Vienna, and in fact I did not
visit the U.S. again until 1945.

Q$_6$: Can you recall the circumstances that led to your working with
Mises?

HAYEK: When I graduated in 1921 there was in Vienna a new temporary office to carry out certain provisions of the peace treaty of
1918—the settlement of prewar private debts between the nations.
Mises, on behalf of the chamber of commerce, was one of the directors of this new office. It was very attractive to new people, because
if a young man had studied law and spoke two foreign languages,
he could get a much better paid position in the circumstances. I was
one of these fortunate men and came—this is again off the record,
but for your amusement—I came to Mises with a letter of introduction from Wieser recommending me for this position. And Mises,
I still can see him before me, reading Wieser's letter of introduction,
looking at me. "Wieser says you're a promising young economist.
I've never seen you at my lectures." Still, he gave me the job, and
so for the next five years—interrupted by a visit to America—I was
working under him, and then I brought back from America a new
idea of great predictions, the sort of thing which the Harvard economic barometer had developed in the 1920s. Mises helped me to
create in the same building an institute for pursuing this type of
research.

Q$_6$: About what year are we talking?

HAYEK: That was the second part of the 1920s. The first part of the 1920s, I worked with him in that office, and from 1927 to 1931 exactly, until I went to London, I was acting as organizer of this institute, beginning just with myself and the secretary and gradually expanding it, getting in Morgenstern as my collaborator, who afterwards took over for me.

The office was engaged in clearing certain private debts between two countries which got blocked by the outbreak of war, debts which had been outstanding for five years, with extremely complicated provisions because of currency changes and so on. . . . By that time I had returned from America; I used to speak French fairly well, and I knew even some Italian, which I had picked up in the war. The three foreign languages, plus law, plus economics, qualified me for what was comparatively a very well paid job. Well paid for a government office, because it was a temporary position; I was not a regular civil servant but a temporary civil servant, with a much higher salary than I would have had. So it was quite an attractive position, even if it hadn't been that Mises became my official head.

I must say a few words here about my curious relation to Ludwig von Mises, from whom later I have probably learnt more than from any other man, but who in the conventional sense was never my teacher. I believe that while I was a regular student I only once went to a lecture of his, but rather disliked him. All that I clearly remember is that when in 1921 I had to call on Mises to apply for a job in the government office of which he then was one of the directors, equipped with a very kind letter of introduction by Wieser in which I was described as one of the more promising younger economists, I had only a vague idea of what kind of person to expect, but was certainly completely unknown to Mises who received (and accepted) the candidate, whom he had never seen at the university, with polite skepticism.

Once I was employed in that office, our contacts rapidly became close, and for the following eight years Mises was unquestionably the personal contact from whom I profited most, not only by way of intellectual stimulation but also for his direct assistance in my career. A most unconventional civil servant (temporary), he soon gave me scope by putting me on new and responsible jobs for which usually much more senior persons would be employed. And when, after only a year and a half [in 1923], I decided that I wanted to go to America for further study, it was he who smoothed my way not only by getting for me the necessary leave of absence but on financial conditions so favorable as to make my plan practicable.

After my return I joined the *Privatseminar* which he held in the evening at his office and which I believe had already been going on for some while before I had left. During the middle twenties, this was much the most important center of economic discussion at Vienna, and it also provided the nucleus for the revised *Nationalökonomisch Gesellschaft* [National Economics Society], which I got going again a little later, after it had been discontinued for a few years, partly with the intention of bridging the growing gap which separated Mises and his group from the group of Hans Mayer at the university.

It was also Mises to whom I owe the creation of the Austrian Institute for Business Cycle Research, conceived by him, I believe, largely for the purpose of providing scope for me after he had failed to get me as a sort of scientific assistant into the chamber of commerce where he held his main job (for the purpose of building up there under his direction an economic research division). It came at a most opportune moment. I had married in the summer of 1926, and my position as a temporary civil servant in the *Abrechnungsamt*, where my wife was also employed, was really satisfactory neither with regard to income nor to prospects. It did not even give me much free time, and I could not much longer have carried on my own studies side by side with my office work at the rate I had done till then.

While the idea of the institute arose out of conversations I had had with Mises about what I had seen of economic research in America, and while he left to me the writing out of the various preparatory memoranda and the details of the organization, it was he who persuaded the various government offices and trade organizations, etc., to provide the funds and to put me in charge. Once [the institute was] established (as of January 1, 1927), Mises continued to give me all help needed but left me a completely free hand in the actual conduct of its affairs.

Q$_6$: You saw, at least, the great German inflation. And did Austria participate in that?

HAYEK: We had it before. The Austrian inflation began almost immediately after the war. At my first job, under Mises, in October 1921, I got a monthly salary of 5,000 old kronen a month. In the next month, I had to be paid three times that in order to be able to live on it. And by next July, it reached one million a month. So my first ten months of professional life were in what then was still regarded as an enormous inflation, but the Germans' two or three years later actually got much higher. At the time, that a currency should depreciate to finally one million being almost the unit was unknown. After the reform, 10,000 became the new unit. That was then a very major inflation.

By the time the German inflation came, we knew all about it. Mises was the only one who taught us a mechanism on it—Mises was the great monetary expert. At that time he was almost exclusively a monetary expert. His book on socialism was yet to come. Only the first essay on the calculation had already appeared. And at one time, I happen to know privately, for your information, Mises had in his drawer all the papers which should have enabled him from moment to moment to take over the finance ministry, which he hoped he would be called for, to stabilize the currency. But he was never called for it. One of the great disappointments of his life. But he finally, seeing that it was politically impossible, had a considerable hand in the League of Nations commission that was sent to Vienna in charge of finance. To what extent he advised the League of Nations commissioner, I do not know, but I suspect that although officially he had no hand with it, the ultimate stabilization was done on his advice.

Q$_6$: On Mises's advice?

HAYEK: He was the only person in Vienna capable to do that.

Q$_6$: There is a story, perhaps apocryphal, that Mises was asked during this inflation how to stop it. And he said, "Meet me at 12 o'clock at this building." And it turned out at 12 midnight they met him at the printing office, where they were printing the money. And they said, "How can we stop this inflation?" And he said, "Hear that noise? Turn it off."

* * *

Q$_6$: Can you tell us about the Mises seminar?

HAYEK: Mises's office was the place of the so-called private seminar that took place at the chamber of commerce during the academic year twice a month.

Q$_6$: This is significant, though. Are you saying that Mises, teaching outside of the university—that students did not get credit for this advanced teaching?

HAYEK: Nothing, it was purely a discussion club.

Q$_6$: Who are some of the people who came, that you remember, or ever heard of, whom we would know, who would be important for us?

HAYEK: First, of an intermediate generation, between Mises's and my own, people were still in the Böhm-Bawerk seminar. A man called Strigl, Richard [von] Strigl, whom we all expected to succeed to the professorship, but who died young, and another man called Schams. Then comes my generation, in which I am slightly the oldest, although I have one contemporary, a lady called Stefanie Browne. She now spells it English; she used to be "Braun," when I knew her in Austria. She is, I believe, the only surviving member of my own age. Used to be another woman of the same age, who was secretary of the bankers' association, Lena Lieser, who has been dead for many years. Then comes Haberler, only a year my junior. Then, to take first the better-known figures, Machlup, who is two years younger; Morgenstern, who is at Princeton; well, you might say it was a total of up to twenty people, of whom about twelve would regularly meet, twice a month, in Mises's actual chamber of commerce office, without any formal connection with the university. All ex-university students, discussing I believe predominantly questions of scientific methodology rather than particular problems. Even if we'd start out with a very practical concrete problem of the time, we'd very soon be off with a conflict between the different groups of economics.

Later, in the early 1930s, during the last four years when they still met, it became a considerable point of attraction for foreign students. That was after I had left. I don't remember, but I know that during the later years, French, English, American students used to come in for a term, take part in these discussions of economics. And during the final years of the Austrian School in Austria, it was the center not only for the Austrian School itself but attracted students from all over the world to join into the discussion. That I knew mainly by hearsay, because I was absolutely the first to leave Vienna, before the emigration in any sense had started. Because I never imagined that I was emigrating. But if at the age of thirty-two you are offered a professorship at the University of London, you take it. I never considered that this was moving myself outside of Austria. It was just the first decisive step in my academic career. It was the world which prevented me from ever returning after this.

Q_6: But your interpretation of Austrian economics did not remain the same as Mises's.

HAYEK: Let me get to the crucial point. What I see only now clearly is the problem of my relation to Mises, which began with my 1937 article on the economics of knowledge, which was an attempt to persuade Mises himself that when he asserted that the market theory was a priori, he was wrong; that what was a priori was only the logic of individual action, but the moment that you passed from this to the interaction of many people, you entered into the empirical field. Curiously enough, while Mises was very resentful of any criticism by his pupils and temporarily broke both with Machlup and Haberler because they had criticized him, he took my critique silently and even approved the article as if he had not been aware that it was a criticism of his own views. I cannot explain this. But my view has come very much further. I believe I can now even explain why what I admit is a masterly critique by Mises of socialism has not been really effective. Because Mises remained in the end himself a rationalist-utilitarian, and with a rationalist-utilitarianism, the rejection of socialism is irreconcilable.

Capitalism presumes that apart from our rational insight we possess a traditional endowment of morals, which has been tested by evolution but not designed by our intelligence. We have never invented private property because we understood these consequences, nor have we ever invented the family. It so happens that these traditions, essentially a religious tradition, and I am as much an agnostic as Mises was, but I must admit that the two decisive traditions which make it possible for us to build up an order which extends our vision cannot be the result of our intellectual insight but must be the result of a moral tradition, which as I now put it is the result of group selection and not of individual selection, something which we can ex post interpret. But Mises's postulate—if we are strictly rational and decide all the bases, we can see that socialism is wrong—is a mistake. If we remain strict rationalists, utilitarians, that implies we can arrange everything according to our pleasure. So Mises never could free himself from that fundamental philosophy, in which we have all grown up, that reason can do everything better than mere habit. From this he could never loose himself. In this respect, although I accept nearly everything of his criticism of socialism, I now understand why it has not been fully effective, because in his case it's still based on the fundamental mistake of rationalism and socialism, that we have the intellectual power to arrange everything rationally, which is now in conflict with the assertion— In one place he says we can't do it, another place he argues, being rational people, we must try to do it.

PART TWO

London

Shortly before I received the invitation to the visiting professorship in London, I had once half jokingly remarked to my wife that if I could plan my career, I should wish now first to go to London as professor, return to Vienna after a few years, first as professor and later as president of the Austrian *Nationalbank*, and finally, when my active work as scholar or administrator was completed, to return to London as Austrian minister. Except for the first step—which was the most unlikely and yet the only one to come true—this was, in the then state of the world, by no means an unreasonable aspiration and would have given me that sort of life on the borderline of purely academic and public work which probably, in the later part of my life, I should have found most satisfactory—even if at times I might have longed for the more complete seclusion of a purely academic life. That in fact I was led into the life almost of a pure scholar was not entirely a matter of inclination and would certainly not have happened if I had stayed in Austria. But transferred into an entirely different environment, my factual knowledge was inevitably so much inferior to that of my colleagues that I got pushed rather further than was entirely to my liking into an entirely theoretical and bookish field.

I understand that I owe the original invitation to deliver four lectures on economic theory at the London School of Economics to the impression which my essay on "The Paradox of Saving" [1931] had made on Lionel Robbins, recently appointed to a professorship there and my very close contemporary and, during my years at London, my most intimate friend. I was most fortunate with regard to the moment the invitation reached me. I had recently conceived an idea concerning the mechanism of industrial fluctuation, which I was able to write out rapidly in the flush of the first excitement but using at the same time the results of my studies in the history of ideas which had occupied me for some time. Though my English was yet hardly adequate for the task (the published version of *Prices and Production* [1931] was extensively revised by Robbins), the lectures were most successful, particularly where I departed from the prepared manuscript. This led to the offer of a visiting professorship for 1931–32, which in time was followed by my regular appointment to the Tooke Professorship of Economic Science and Studies, which I held from 1932 to the end of 1949.

Q$_6$: What I want to know is, you were invited to be a professor at the London School of Economics, but why wasn't Mises invited? He couldn't speak English?

HAYEK: By that time, 1931, Mises was still a relatively minor figure confined to a particular field. The man had done two things: a theory of money, and a criticism of socialism. His great book, his philosophical essay, came out even in German only in 1938, and the American version only in the 1940s. That established him as a great social philosopher. But by the early 1930s, Mises was internationally—so far as he was known at all, which was limited—known to people like Robbins as a man who had done a distinctive contribution to the theory of money, developing Menger and developing most effectively his criticism of socialism.

I had done a thing which none of the others had done. I had before the beginning of the Rockefeller fellowships in 1923 on my own risk come to America, spent fifteen months in America, was in consequence speaking fluent English. That's number one. It's not the whole story. That was a precondition. Mises could hardly have taken the time, and certainly none of my other colleagues. Then, too, I had while in America devoted a lot of time to the criticism of the peculiar kind of American underconsumption analysis—which was very similar to what Keynes later produced—by Foster and Catchings; I don't know if you still remember these names. I had spent a great deal of time and was absolutely ready to criticize any underconsumption theory. When Keynes then produced his, I pounced upon him completely equipped.

I was working during all the 1920s on this sort of problem. I had started on writing a great treatise on money, which I never completed but for which I'd proposed to start with ten chapters on the history of monetary theory and policy, of which, by the end of the 1920s, I'd written the first four chapters dealing with the developments in England between 1690 and 1900. So when I came to London it turned out that I knew much more about the history of English monetary theory than any of the English professors themselves, which caused a great impression.

When I gave in Vienna my initial lectures as *Privatdozent,* I chose for my subject this kind of underconsumption theory which had then become acute in England. And Robbins could read German. That's an almost unique factor, an English professor who could read German literature—that's good luck, that he pounced on my subject: This is the thing we need at the moment, to fight Keynes. So I was called in for this purpose, produced of course a lecture which was original, which suggested more knowledge of the history of English theory than anybody else. Was sympathetically received by Robbins, who had been influenced by the Austrian school. We at once understood each other. This combination of accidents led to my appointment in London. It was luck from beginning to end.

Q$_6$: But it was *Prices and Production* which brought the Austrian trade cycle theory to the attention of our world.

HAYEK: Yes, and that was equally accidental. The invitation reached me when I had for the first time a clear picture of this theory but had not yet gone into all the complicated details. If I had progressed in working out an elaborate treatise, I would have encountered any number of complications and would have produced a very difficult treatise. The invitation met me at the moment where I could just quickly tell the story as a general survey, as I then saw it.

To give you the main illustration, from my simple exposition I could operate with a grave simplification in Böhm-Bawerk, operating with an average period of production. The average period of production is a beautiful simplification, but doesn't help you at all. I became aware later that the question of a single average period of production was a complex structure; if I had been aware of this in

1931, I could not have given a beautiful simple exposition, but I could have confused everybody. Since I was not yet aware of the difficulties, I gave these incredibly successful lectures; but it was not really their own merit, it was the situation in which this particular set of lectures hit London. I expected nothing less than that four lectures I gave in London would lead to an invitation. Of course in the first instance it only produced an invitation for a visiting professorship for one year. But I fitted in so well and Robbins and I became very close friends, we worked beautifully together, and from 1931 till 1940 we were thinking together and working together. Then I'm afraid he fell under Keynes's influence.

On arriving for the first one-year appointment in 1931 (on the day after the devaluation of the pound, of which I learnt on passing through Paris), we had taken a furnished house in the Hampstead Garden Suburb (in Constable Close, close to the Robbinses) and remained in that neighborhood—from 1932 to 1939 in a rented house (15 Turner Close), and from 1939 in one nearby (8 Turner Close), which I bought. There were quite a group of the LSE economists living in the Garden suburb at the time—apart from the Robbinses, who became our closest friends, Arnold Plant, Frank Paish, George Schwarz, and later for a time James Meade.

We lived very quietly with very little social life beyond the occasional entertaining of a visiting colleague. We were of course still running the house with the help of a regular maid. These were usually Austrian girls, one of whom stayed with us for a long time and became quite a member of the family. But this was about all that the then salary of a professor (at first £1,000 per annum, after five years £1,250) would support. Until 1936 we did without a car, and the one indulgence I granted myself was the membership in the Reform Club, which became very important to me and by now is the only "home" I have known for close to forty years.

In my early years in London, my interest remained concentrated on the theory of money, capital, and industrial fluctuations, and my main goal became soon a restatement of the theory of capital as a foundation for a more satisfactory account of the dynamic phenomena. I found the restatement of the theory of capital without the simplifications employed by my predecessors extremely difficult, but stuck to it till I felt I was getting stale and finally published what was really only a part of the planned work in 1941 as *The Pure Theory of Capital*, under the pretext that otherwise the war might make completion of the work impossible. But I never really started on the intended monetary or dynamic continuation. Though I tried hard to concentrate further on this subject, my interest began to wander to other topics.

It was still more or less an accident when in 1935, in editing various essays on socialist planning, I contributed myself two fairly long essays to it. But I got increasingly interested in the philosophical and methodological questions which, I came to be more and more convinced, were ultimately responsible for some of the current political differences. The decisive step in this development of my thinking was the paper on "Economics and Knowledge," which I read in 1936 as the presidential address to the London Economic Club. Together with some later related papers reprinted with it in *Individualism and Economic Order* [1948], this seems to me in retrospect the most original contribution I have made to the theory of economics.

Q₅: I'd like to shift, if I could, to your basic political theory— political philosophy—position. I'd like to ask you a bit of intellectual history here, in terms of your own position. We both started out, more or less, as technical economists, and then became interested in more political-philosophical questions. Could you trace for us the evolution of your own thinking in that respect?

HAYEK: It really began with my doing that volume on collectivist economic planning, which was originally merely caused by the fact that I found that certain new insights which were known on the Continent had not reached the English-speaking world yet. It was largely Mises and his school, but also certain discussions by Barone and others, which were then completely unknown to the English-speaking world. Being forced to explain this development on the Continent in the introduction and the conclusion to this volume, which contained translations, I was curiously enough driven not only into political philosophy but into an analysis of the methodological misconceptions of economics. [These misconceptions] seemed to me to lead to these naive conceptions of "After all, what the market does we can do better intellectually." My way from there was very largely around methodological considerations, which led me back to— I think the decisive event was that essay I did in about 1937 on "Economics and Knowledge."

Q_5: That was a brilliant essay.

HAYEK: I think that was the decisive point of the change in my outlook. As I would put it now, [it elaborated] the conception that prices serve as guides to action and must be explained in determining what people ought to do—they're not determined by what people have done in the past.

But, of course, psychologically the consequence of the whole model of marginal-utility analysis was perhaps the decisive point which, as I now see the whole thing—the market as a system of the utilization of knowledge, which nobody can possess as a whole, which only through the market situation leads people to aim at the needs of people whom they do not know, make use of facilities for which they have no direct information; all this condensed in abstract signals, and that our whole modern wealth and production could arise only thanks to this mechanism—is, I believe, the basis not only of my economic but also much of my political views. It reduces the possible task of authority very much if you realize that the market has in that sense a superiority, because the amount of information the authorities can use is always very limited, and the market uses an infinitely greater amount of information than the authorities can ever do.

During the nine or ten months of every year we lived in London, the main center of my activities was of course the LSE. While I did most of my scientific work at home in the morning and most of my teaching in the afternoon and evening, I would usually leave home about 11 A.M. and lunch at the school, or occasionally at the club. The senior common room at the school was then an extraordinarily interesting group and still of a size which made it possible to know most of the members well. It was always a place of lively discussion; in the later 1930s, chiefly about the changing political developments of the world. In spite of the sharp political differences between a leftish majority and the (in the old sense) liberal or conservative economists and lawyers, the atmosphere was always very friendly.

I believe that the total teaching staff was then not much in excess of one hundred, yet it included a quite extraordinary array of great talents and conversational gifts. Apart from the economists already mentioned (to whom I ought to add Theodore Gregory, John Hicks, and Frederic Benham), there were Harold Laski and Denis Brogan as the best talkers, Tawney and Eileen Power, Malinowski, and of course the director, Sir William Beveridge, and the secretary of the school, Mrs. Mair, as the most prominent members. During my early years, two of the retired old professors, Edwin Cannan and Graham Wallas, still occasionally appeared and so did Sidney (and on a few occasions Beatrice) Webb.

In some ways it is these years in London before the war which in retrospect seem to me the intellectually most active and satisfying of my life. I certainly never again could arouse the same passionate interest in the technicalities of theoretical economics or profit in the same way from discussion with first-class minds with similar interests. Especially the seminar—which was really conducted by Robbins but for which I nominally shared responsibility with him—taught me more economics than anything else.

Q6: The London School of Economics was originally a Fabian institution. How was it that by 1931 you and Robbins were both on the faculty?

HAYEK: I suppose it was wholly due to the person of Edwin Cannan. The Webbs were in this sense very decent. They wanted a good theoretician who was an independent mind, and were so convinced that unprejudiced study of economics must lead to socialism, that they made the mistake of accepting someone who wouldn't [agree with that conclusion] at all. And Cannan, who was the main professor, and Foxwell, who had the professorship of money and banking, were completely separated from the Fabian part. . . . [I]n a way Laski and I had something in common—we were both great book collectors—but apart from this we had of course nothing in common at all. We hardly spoke the same language. Don't ask me to begin to tell you stories about LSE—because of this extraordinary person Harold Laski, it was a most peculiar place.

Q$_6$: Perhaps one or two?

HAYEK: Harold Laski was a pathological problem. Even among his friends today, they recognize he was a pathological liar. If you have time, I'll tell you one or two stories, just from our book-collecting experience. You know book collectors are like fishermen—they always have found something unique. But Harold Laski took the following forms: Would come one midday, when we always met after lunch in the senior common room, enthusiastic; just been to Charing Cross Road, and in one of these boxes there were some beautiful French duodecimal volumes of the eighteenth century. He turned them over, all religious stuff. Suddenly found that the back of one was thicker than the other. So Laski asked him, "And how much is it?" "Sixpence each." So he put down a shilling, took the two volumes, slit one open, and out fell four letters exchanged between Rousseau and Voltaire. They were never published. But that was typical for the man.

Q$_6$: He just made the story up?

HAYEK: Completely. Later, there are two memorable occasions. Even before we moved to Cambridge in 1939 in preparation for the probable outbreak of war, as in 1940, before we'd all moved, before the bombing in London. Both Laski and I were spending the evenings of the days we were teaching—we were coming up from London for two days a week—in the house of a colleague, Lancelot Beales. The first occasion was really very remarkable because Harold Laski was entertaining us, lecturing about the beauties of the Russian system, and was interrupted by the announcement of the news. We were all listening to the BBC, I believe, at half past seven, and the news came through of the Stalin-Ribbentrop pact, and afterwards Laski behaved as if he had never in his life said a good word about the Bolsheviks, the most abominable creatures ever. He didn't seem to remember what he had said for the preceding twenty years of his life. But a year later, in exactly the same position, again sitting together after dinner listening to the news, Harold had just been to his home, Manchester, and had experienced the first bombing attack. On that occasion he'd been very shaken, because one bomb had fallen close to his hotel and badly shaken him. Three weeks later when I heard of this story again, it had his hotel being hit and him falling with his bed four floors into the cellar.

Q_6: The London School: Were the students mostly Fabians, or were they just normal students trying to get a degree? What was the motivation to come to the LSE in the 1930s?

HAYEK: You have to distinguish between faculty and students. On the faculty there was an enormous difference between economists on the one hand and political scientists and sociologists on the other. In between there were the lawyers, the geographers, the economic historians, who were either neutral or, you could say, the usual type would be a very mild Fabian. People of the Bloomsbury group, people like Eileen Power, who stuck in the Bloomsbury group. Very nice and decent people in their way, not doctrinaire.

Q_6: I had no idea Eileen Power was connected with Bloomsbury.

HAYEK: Oh yes; she happened to live there. The Bloomsbury people were all her neighbors; she knew them all in this way. I don't think she was any active—but they were all very familiar to her. And Tawney, who was of course all very Fabian, but a man you could talk with, not doctrinaire, very interesting man; personally I liked Tawney. Harold Laski was almost a joke, and I could never take Harold Laski, but at that time people took him seriously. Now even his party fellows, even before his death, do not take him seriously as a thinker. He must have been as a very young man very brilliant, but by the time I knew him he was not.

Q_6: And the LSE director, Beveridge?

HAYEK: As for Beveridge, he was completely ignorant of any economics whatever.

Q_6: He was a public servant, primarily.

HAYEK: Yes, he was a public servant. His career, I think, was most successful when he was a leader writer for *The Morning Post*. He could write to any subject where he was given instruction.

Q_6: I suppose that's somehow connected with the Oxford tutorial system, in which one is expected to write a very, very good essay on a different subject every week. One can mug it up and then completely forget it, without having any continuing line of thought or any background theoretical interest.

HAYEK: But he was an extreme. I've never met anybody who was so able to write about things of which he had no knowledge. Another story about Beveridge, which I've told many times. He had fortunately acquired the habit, when he spoke publicly about economic subjects, to get either Lionel Robbins or me to read the draft. On one occasion, one of his lectures was so outrageously inflationist that I gave him a tutorial. Fortunately, I saw the next draft, which contained the sentence, "But unfortunately, as Professor Hayek has discovered, an increase in the quantity of money tends to drive up prices."

Q_6: So it was not only Keynes who, as you wrote, had gaps in his knowledge.

HAYEK: It turned out that the LSE economists, and even Lionel Robbins, had not had a classical education. There was a time when I concluded every departmental committee meeting by saying, *"Beveridge delendus est."* I found out that not one of them understood what I was saying. It's a famous phrase, a story from, I believe, Cicero. *Ceterum censeo Catonum esse delendum.* It was his argumentation against Cato; and he is supposed to have concluded every speech in the Senate with, "Thus I believe that we must destroy Cato."

I assumed this to be popular knowledge and used this phrase against Beveridge, because I found him quite impossible. The general irresponsibility of the man, which got the school into serious difficulty. He would get money from Rockefeller for one purpose and spend it on a different one, and brought the school in awful discredit. His momentary enthusiasms. I believe he had got a lot of money—I forget from what in this instance—for building a new library, and then used it to appoint Lancelot Hogben in sociobiology. That was a famous episode, which is long forgotten. When the rumor went around that when Hogben arrived, cages would be erected on the floor of the lower front part of the LSE building, where chimpanzees would be kept in order to study their mating habits, it caused great excitement amongst the students. Hogben was a not uninteresting person; in fact, he was a very difficult person.

PLATES

1. From the Hayek family photo album: "In this room, in the Messenhausergasse at the corner of Landstrasse Hauptstrasse, on May 8, 1899, Fritz Hayek was born." Translated from notation in his mother's script.

2. Josef von Hayek, who was enobled in 1789 at age 39, adding the "von" to the family name.

3. Hayek's paternal great-grandfather Heinrich von Hayek, son of Josef.

4. Franziska von Hayek (née Zwierzina), wife of Heinrich von Hayek, and her son Gustav, about 1850.

5. Hayek's maternal grandfather
Franz von Juraschek.

6. Johanna Stallner, first wife of
Franz von Juraschek.

7. Hayek's father August Edler von Hayek (1871–1928).

8. Hayek as a child in Vienna, 1903.

9. Hayek on the balcony at Draschepark with his brother Erich, 1904.

10. Hayek and his brother Heinz in Biedermeier dress, about to leave for dancing class, 1911.

11. The family, which habitually spent Sundays together, gathered for the sixtieth birthday of Hayek's maternal grandfather Franz von Juraschek, February 25, 1909. From l. to r., standing, Hayek's mother Felicitas (née von Juraschek); Ida (née Pokorny) von Juraschek (second wife to Franz); the honoree. Seated, August von Hayek (Hayek's father); Erich von Hayek (Hayek's brother); Fritz von Hayek; Franz von Juraschek (his uncle); Gertrud von Juraschek (his aunt); Heinz von Hayek (Hayek's brother); and Greta von Juraschek (his aunt).

12. About 1911, all three Hayek brothers (Erich, Heinz, and Fritz). His mother noted, "The last time our big Fritz wore a sailor suit."

13. On the customary summer holiday in the country, this time near Schladming, the three boys (Fritz, Heinz, and Erich) with their mother. Most of Hayek's summers for the rest of his life were spent in the Austrian Tyrol.

14. Two photos from the summer holiday of 1916. Hayek is nearing maturity. "Despite the war, we had a pleasant summer stay," his mother wrote under the pictures. a) Erich, Heinz, and Fritz with their mother. b) Resting after a swim.

15. Age 19, Hayek serves as an artillery spotter on the Italian front at the Piave River, 1918.

16. Hayek as an officer in the Austrian Army, 1918.

17. A formal portrait of Hayek in the regalia of the Austrian Army, Vienna, 1918.

18. Photographed on his father's fiftieth birthday in 1921, Hayek already held a doctoral degree from the University of Vienna.

19. Hayek (in deck chair) on the steamer returning to Vienna after his initial period of independent study in New York, 1924. Note his beard.

20. At Gaschurn, with his first child Christine, 1932.

21. Lionel Robbins, Hayek's neighbor in Hampstead and departmental colleague at the London School of Economics, 1949.

22. Hayek and economist Fritz Machlup at Beloit College, circa 1960.

23. Hayek, Ludwig von Mises, and Fritz Machlup at a dinner in von Mises's honor, New York, March 7, 1956.

24. Hayek completing *The Constitution of Liberty* in the Alps, 1958.

25. Hayek in his study in 1960, during the University of Chicago years (1950–62).

26. Viennese physicist Erwin Schrödinger (1887–1961).

27. With Lionel Robbins at the wedding of Hayek's son Laurence, 1961. A friendship was resumed after the interval of the Chicago years.

28. Analogy Symposium, Villa Serbelloni, Bellagio, Italy, April 17–24, 1966.
Bruno Leoni, Ardry, Matson, Hayek, John Watkins, R. Jung, Hyden,
Paul Feyerabend.

But on the whole I got on with all the difficult persons; until a certain clash with Mannheim, I even got on quite well with Laski. Until he got in his mind that *The Road to Serfdom* was written against him. After that, it ended; but since we were both passionate book collectors, we had a good bit in common.

But I regarded Beveridge as a real danger for the school. Of course, there is the famous episode in which he nearly took over the Frankfurt School—

Q₆: Oh yes; that was he who did that. I hadn't got that connection.

HAYEK: Oh yes. It was stopped only at the very last moment.

Q₆: I know you had told me about stopping it. I hadn't realized it was Beveridge who had done it.

HAYEK: You find the story in Lionel Robbins's autobiography. Robbins had a good instinct, but he knew very little about this affair; he came in, literally, when the contract was lying for signature on Beveridge's table. Thank God, he wouldn't swallow this stuff. "But they are excellent." Then he called me in to tell Beveridge what the situation was. It would have been a catastrophe if the LSE had been absorbed. But a great temptation was the marvelous library which they had, which they were going to bring with them; and Beveridge couldn't resist it, which brought him to the point of signing this.

It was only one of many things. He was absolutely unpredictable. It was not only he, it was the extraordinary lady who later became Lady Beveridge. You never heard of her? Oh, you knew nothing of the London School of Economics if you didn't know who Mrs. Mair was. English; Scottish. She was the wife of a civil servant [and] had herself been in the civil service with Beveridge in the Ministry of Food. When Beveridge became director of the London School of Economics, he took her with him. She really dominated affairs. She was a crude, energetic woman who knew what she wanted; completely dominated him. Another famous episode, which is so characteristic: They were reputed to have a sexual relationship. I'm sure nothing of the sort. There was an occasion when, as frequently happened, this energetic, cold woman came up in the senior common room, indignant about Beveridge not making up his mind in the right direction. And finally she burst out, "He isn't man enough; he isn't man enough. I know."

It was this pair which became fairly intolerable, and it was completely unpredictable what he would do next and how he would discredit the school. For a time his money-raising skill had been extraordinarily successful, but discrediting by the way he used the money for different purposes than it was raised for—not that he was dishonest, he was perfectly honest, but his enthusiasm shifted, and he felt he was completely entitled to use the money for what he regarded at the moment as the best purposes. I was agitating against him in my later years at LSE; and I had the lowest possible opinion about his— Very difficult what term to use. I can't say "intellectual qualities." He was a marvelous expositor. He had the gift of making it lead to any bridge you gave him. One of the classic illustrations was, as soon as I arrived at LSE, Beveridge and his professors had just published a little book in favor of free trade. Then the change in government occurred, and in my presence Beveridge said to Robbins, "Now it's time to write a book in favor of protection."

Q_6: He wasn't a member of your seminar, I suppose.

HAYEK: No, he wasn't the least interested in economics. He knew no economics whatever. In this case you can take it literally. I sometimes say the same of Keynes, but in fact they were different. Keynes knew his own economics and was intelligent enough to construct a theory. Beveridge did not have that quality. He was a perfect barrister, could make a case for a brief that was presented to him.

Q_6: I know Kaldor was a member of your seminar and was closely associated with you at one time. How did he leave you for Beveridge and Keynes? Is there some story there?

HAYEK: Difficult to say. You know, he was one of the translators of my *Geldtheorie und Konjunkturtheorie*, he and a very nice young woman [H. M. Croome] who died young. He occasionally freely admitted that in his beginnings he was a Hayekian. I think it was Keynes's *Treatise* [1930] which convinced him, and got him around to the other side. And he worked closely with Beveridge. He wrote Beveridge's book on employment. That's quite a well-known fact. What economics is there is purely Kaldor's. Beveridge would have been entirely unable to write such a book. In that book there was an essay which was admittedly by Kaldor, but the whole thing is by him. That essay was just one that Beveridge didn't want to commit to, because he couldn't understand it.

Q_6: It seems that both Beveridge and Kaldor then made their political careers on the basis of this Keynesianism which they had adopted.

HAYEK: Yes. Kaldor became as a result of this the political/economic advisor either to the prime minister or the minister of finance at that time. They [Kaldor and Balogh] were, as we used to call them, Buda and Pest.

Q_6: Kaldor was Buda.

HAYEK: The comic thing is that both Buda and Pest—nobody doubted who was who. Balogh was Pest. Kaldor was fat and seemed to look like Buddha, and Balogh was so universally disliked that he was Pest.

At another extreme, there was John Hicks. The super intellect; wonderful theoretician, who was really sometimes presumptuous, but I also think there was sometimes justification in it with John Hicks. On one occasion, to my surprise, he said to me, "Oh well, we two understand it." There is a sort of slight intellectual arrogance there. He admitted me as fully his equal, in my own right; but not quite up to his standards. He certainly was the best mind we had, there's no question about that. A very educated, widely read man, with a very good education. Historically well informed.

* * *

Q_2: What is your evaluation of Hicks's book *Value and Capital?*

HAYEK: Oh, really, absolutely first-class work in his time. So far as there is a theory of value proper, which does not extend beyond this and which doesn't really analyze it in terms of directing production, I think it's the final formulation of the theory of value. I don't think Samuelson's improvements are really improvements beyond it. I think the Hicksian analysis in terms of rates of substitution, in that narrow field, is a definite achievement.

Q_2: Do you think that what is now called the Keynesian revolution should have been called the Hicksian revolution? Was he influential in getting Keynes's ideas accepted?

HAYEK: I certainly don't think of Hicks as a revolutionary. I think he tried to give it a more acceptable form. But I have reason to say that it probably should be called a Kaldorian revolution, not for anything which is connected with Kaldor's name, but what spread it was really Lord Beveridge's book on full employment, and that was written by Kaldor and not by Beveridge, because Lord Beveridge never understood any economics.

Almost as soon as I took up my position at London, I got engaged into a controversy with J. M. Keynes, which did much to make me more widely known. (Incidentally, though I continued to disagree with Keynes and had some heated debates with him, we remained personally on the best of terms, and I had in many respects the greatest admiration and liking for him as a man.) Robbins had asked me to review for *Economica* Keynes's recently published *Treatise,* and the first installment of my long review article appeared in the issue of August 1931, just before I took up my position at the London School of Economics. I still believe it was a fairly effective criticism, though it has lost its relevance because Keynes so soon completely changed the ideas.

Keynes's immediate reaction is best described in the words of the late Professor A. C. Pigou, who refers to the episode (without mentioning names) in *Economics in Practice:* "A year or two ago, after the publication of an important book, there appeared an elaborate and careful critique of a number of passages in it. The author's answer was, not to rebut the criticism, but to attack with violence another book, which the critic had himself written several years before. Body-line bowling. The methods of the duello. That kind of thing is surely a mistake."

The thesis on which I started work while I was registered as a Ph.D. student in New York University (I believe I proposed to call it "Is a stabilization of the value of money compatible with its function?")—although neither it nor the German work into which I turned it during the following years in Vienna were ever completed—was in many ways the beginning of a continuous development, of which most of my publications during the next two years are rather by-products or statements of partial results suggested by a particular occasion.

One of the first conclusions at which I remember I had arrived towards the end of 1923 was that stabilisation of national price levels and stabilization of foreign exchange were conflicting aims. But before I could anywhere submit for publication the short article I had written on the subject, I found that Keynes had just stated the same contention in his *Tract on Monetary Reform* [1923]. Lest anybody think that this disappointment in my hope of having made an original discovery is responsible for my later persistent opposition to Keynes, I should add that Keynes was then, and remained for a good deal longer, one of my heroes, and that I greatly admired this particular work of his. I first met him a few years later, on one of my early visits to London, at a meeting of the European institutes concerned with research on industrial fluctuations (I believe, in 1929). We had our first letter clash then; I do not remember about what particular detail of monetary theory where I disagreed. He first attempted, as he often did, to steamroller me into submission— but as soon as I stood up against him and was able to produce a tolerable defense of my view, he began to treat me with respect and has done so ever after, however violently he disagreed with me. (I very much doubt, however, H. J. Laski's story that Keynes once described me as "the most distinguished muddlehead in Europe." This sounds much more like Laski than like Keynes.)

Q₆: When did you first meet Keynes?

HAYEK: I met him first in 1928, before I had any formal contact with the LSE. I went through what was the London and Cambridge Economic Services, which was the beginning of these trade-cycle observation things, involving both London and Cambridge.

I had been the first to organize a meeting of *Konjunkturinstituten* in Vienna, and then London repeated this and of course invited me. Keynes was a member of the board. We at once had a conflict, very friendly, about rate of interest. Inevitably. He did, in his usual manner, try to go like a steamroller over the young man. But the moment—I must grant him this—the moment I stood up with serious arguments, he took me seriously and ever since respected me. I know his general way of talking about me: "Of course he is crazy, but his ideas are also rather interesting." So that was his view about me.

And later we have so many other common interests. Let me tell you the one main story, a thing I very much blame him for. I had reviewed the *Treatise* at great length. I was prepared to criticize it because I had just before done a major piece which had amounted really to a general refutation of the employment function, the direct dependence of employment on the aggregate amount. I thought I had destroyed the whole thing, in the person of Messrs. Foster and Catchings.

There was in the 1920s an American group which had developed in a naive form something very like Keynesian ideas. While I was in America in 1923 and 1924, Messrs. Foster and Catchings offered a prize for the best critique of their work. I did not take the opportunity to prepare one, but the book which received the prize was so poor I thought I must belatedly return to the subject. This lecture, later published in English under the name "The Paradox of Saving," really contains the beginning of my ideas on prices and production.

So when the *Treatise* came out, I was a little annoyed that just then, when I hoped I'd finally demolished the relation between aggregate demand and employment, it was taken up again. It was essentially my first year in England. The review of Keynes's *Treatise* was written in two sections. Incidentally, I think a certain volume of the *Treatise* is much better than *The General Theory* [1936], so it was on the whole quite complimentary, although it criticized the main point. The theory was out, so when the second part came out, Keynes told me, "Oh, never mind; I no longer believe all that." Which is very discouraging.

Q₆: Very discouraging indeed; there's no point to having done it.

HAYEK: In retrospect I always say it was for this reason that I did not return to the charge on *The General Theory*, which is not quite correct. I knew that there was something more fundamental than the difference on this crucial point, but the concepts of this difference, between macro- and micro-theory, had then not yet become quite clear. I was only becoming aware of the fact that really it would have to be discussion of the contrasts between micro- and macro-theory.

But much more important, I had been criticized for the fact that in *Prices and Production* I had a very inadequate theory of capital; that in this crude Böhm-Bawerkian form of an average period of production, it was inadequate. So I had started writing a great book on capital and money, which ultimately dealt with the money phenomenon. It took me very much longer than I thought; I worked seven years on the thing. I was dead tired of the subject before I got to the monetary aspects. And then war came, which finally persuaded me to put that part into a separate volume [*The Pure Theory of Capital*, 1941] and leave for the time being the monetary part altogether, which I was intending to do another time.

It may surprise you, but during the war I was fighting on Keynes's side against his critics, because Keynes was very much afraid of inflation. I actually had published one or two essays, one reviewing his wartime pamphlet and another one on the problem of combatting inflation, which he already approved. During the war years, the great danger had become inflation, no longer deflation; so we were up against inflation. And in these circumstances, where I wanted to strengthen his influence against the inflationists, I did not want to continue the book.

We had become very friendly, because we shared so many other interests, historical and outside economics. On the whole, when we met, we stopped talking economics. I used to meet him fairly frequently during the war, although he was of course working in London, but during the weekends he came back to Cambridge, and I was of course at King's College. So we became personally very great friends, including [his wife] Lydia Lopokova.

On the last occasion, about which I want to speak, I'm not sure whether the two things or three things I want to tell you about happened on the same evening, as I believe, or it may have been two successive evenings. He had recently come back from this extremely exhausting negotiation about the postwar loan in Britain. I'm speaking of six weeks before he died in 1946; at the beginning of the new year. Nevertheless, at high table he entertained us the whole evening on the state of Elizabethan book collecting in America.

Later in the evening, the following happened—and this needs an introductory explanation. He had during the war begun regularly sending to me the *Journal of the History of Ideas,* which was then new; he was the only subscriber to it in England. When he had noticed (this is illustrative of our relationship) that I was interested, as soon as he had read it, he sent it on to me. It so happened that I had received two or three weeks before, but had read the same morning, an article on the conditions of the publication of the lost second work of Copernicus. But I happened to have coffee at King's

College, to sit opposite an astronomer, who might have been frightfully difficult to establish contact with, but I having read this, which he didn't know, he was frightfully interested; so I was telling him all I could remember of the condition of that publication. Keynes was sitting three seats down the way, engaged in another conversation; yet he was listening to our conversation all the time, because he suddenly said, "You're wrong, Hayek," and was able to correct me. It must have been at least two weeks since he had read it, because he sent it to me two weeks before. He was thinking about something else, but he was sufficiently awake and aware to notice. He was right. I hadn't seen that particular detail, but he was able to correct me.

Certainly on the same evening when this happened—perhaps not the same evening when he talked about Elizabethan book collecting in America, but certainly within a few weeks—we still sat together reading newspapers in the senior commons room. I mentioned what Mrs. Robinson and Kahn were doing on monetary policy. He burst out, "They are just fools. You know, my ideas were frightfully important in the 1930s. There was no question of combatting inflation. But you can trust me, Hayek, my ideas have become dated. I'm going to turn public opinion around like this [snapping his fingers]." Six weeks later he was dead. I think he might have done it.

Q_6: He might have; he was a great manipulator of public opinion, wasn't he?

HAYEK: Yes. That was his great conceit. He always called himself a Cassandra. He was convinced he could play public opinion like an instrument. The effect he had on the peace treaties had really gone to his head. Of course he was very conscious of his power over the language, which I'm afraid *The General Theory* doesn't show, but he could write beautifully, and he was a very good speaker. I always said—others don't seem to have mentioned it so much—his voice was so bewitching. He had a very musical voice. I can see that people got enchanted by merely listening to his words.

And the width of his interests. You could talk with him about very many things. There were of course extraordinary gaps in his knowledge. His knowledge was aesthetically guided, with the result that he was completely ignorant of nineteenth-century economic history. Totally ignorant. He just disliked it.

I had to tell him every day, not so much about economic history, but even about the earlier English economists. He knew his Marshall, but very little else. He had had to at one stage take an interest in Malthus, but I had to tell him about Henry Thornton. Much later I realized—I never had an opportunity to tell him this—if I had introduced him to English inflationists of the nineteenth century, that might have put him off.

Q$_6$: Did he know Jevons, do you recall?

HAYEK: Yes. He did know that.

Q$_6$: One would have expected him to. Jevons and also his father wrote books on logic that were—

HAYEK: Yes, his knowledge of Jevons was not so much the economics but the logic. He did know the great discovery and the price index, on the economic side. But the marginal utility—and in particular Jevons had been excellent on capital, which Keynes had no idea of.

   He had hardly anything about international trade theory. He picked out public-impact statistics criteria, which he studied; and if you take his time of study, I don't think he spent more than a year learning economics. His two parts of the tripos, one was mathematics, I believe, and the other was economics. I like to say, I liked Keynes and in many ways admired him, but do not think he was a good economist.

Q$_6$: Late in his life, sometime I think in the 1940s, he was writing an essay about, I think, some aspect of Elizabethan literature, and he was remarking on how short term his memory was. He said, "This week I'm an expert on this subject, and next week I shall know nothing about it at all."

HAYEK: That fits completely. There were single events which surprised me. He was basically very doctrinaire, but had an open mind for a new idea. When I sent him my essay on investment that increases the demand for new capital, he freely admitted it was completely new to him: "But you are probably right." Similarly, when I sent him an essay I did on some sort of stabilization; I forget the term now. There was a proposal at that time for stabilizing the currency in terms of an index number [commodity-reserve currency]. He entered into the thing, didn't quite fit into the thing, with full interest. Again in this instance, the antecedents of this idea were completely strange to him.

Q_6: At what point did you begin to realize that Keynes had won the battle temporarily, that he had got his views accepted by those who were making decisions in government and elsewhere?

HAYEK: That he definitely won? Only after the war.

Q_6: After the war. I don't mean the theoretical battle; I mean the practical battle, in connection with governments.

HAYEK: Which is a little connected with one other aspect, that Keynes had got Lionel Robbins around, as a result of working together in government circles during the war.

Q_6: They were working together; I see.

HAYEK: Oh, yes; they were together at Bretton Woods as British representatives. And Lionel, who was very anti-Keynesian before the war, was more or less won over by him. Not so much on pure theoretical argument, but he was, I'm afraid—there's another story I better tell you now. I've a theory that all economists who serve in government are corrupted as a result of serving in government. And I admit even (that's what I might insert here) that I owe my own independence [to the fact] that I cleared out of every country as soon as they started using me for governmental service.

Q_6: I was about to ask you about that.

HAYEK: I was once sitting on a governmental committee in Austria; six weeks or six months later I was out. I had not been used [in Britain] during the wartime. I was still the ex-alien, enemy alien; I had a very privileged position, you see. I was not used for any war purposes, but I was not molested. It couldn't have been a more ideal position in England. But after the war I did one thing, a very curious thing—I did a social survey of Gibraltar.

There was trouble—1944, in the last year of the war—there was a trouble with dock workers. As is of course the tradition, the dock workers brought from England were paid more than the Gibraltarian dock workers, and there was trouble about this. There didn't even exist an index of the cost of living, so the Colonial Office appealed to me, could I get them a good student that could go to Gibraltar to do a cost-of-living index. I said, "There are no good students now; I haven't any students. But if you want me to go to Gibraltar, I can do it during my vacation and enjoy it." "If you go, we will ask you to do more. Can you do a social survey of Gibraltar?"

So I went for six weeks to Gibraltar, which was extraordinary— again, don't tempt me to tell you anecdotes about this; it would be endless. Anyhow, I did my stint of government service, but it was the last one. Next time the Colonial Office asked me to go to Cyprus for them, I had to say no, I'm afraid I've committed myself to go to America.

So it was not long enough to be corrupted. In America it never got quite as far. The first time they asked me to sit on a committee in Washington, I had to say, no, I'm leaving. So I have been spared practical experience with government service. And watching, in the case of a man I so much admired like Lionel Robbins, I've no doubt that corrupts the attitude of the economist. He becomes a statesman instead of an economist.

Q_6: I suppose it's a choice: one or the other. And there's very little way to do both.

HAYEK: Keynes of course in a way was much more the statesman.

Q_6: Much more than a theoretician.

HAYEK: But Robbins, I wanted to add (I wish you could talk with him yourself), one has to be aware of one extremely likable habit. He's the most loyal friend of anyone you can meet. But if he were asked his memories of Harold Laski, or Beveridge, it would be honest, but it would not be true. Much embellished. Because they were close friends of his. I'm afraid I am much more open in this sort of thing. I don't keep my mouth shut; my stories about Laski and Beveridge can be rather malicious.

If you were to ask me, who were the most interesting people with whom you would love to spend an evening again, it would be the two economists, Schumpeter and Keynes, who had certain things in common. In one phrase I can put it: *pour épater les bourgeois.* Both were this, in a different way. Schumpeter is a greater scholar than Keynes, and a more brilliant intellect. There was a most impressive quickness with which he would see a point. Yet he had a complete lack of a really coherent philosophy. He trusted his intuitions. I don't think there ever really can be a good biography of this, because it would need a close friend who was critical also, and I don't think there is such a person.

* * *

Q_6: Could you say something about your differences with Keynesian economists?

HAYEK: Keynes, against his intentions, had stimulated the development of macroeconomics. I was convinced that not only his particular conclusions but the whole foundation of macroeconomics was wrong, so I wanted to demonstrate that we had to return to microeconomics. The macroeconomic approach came from the natural scientists, that one could deduce anything for measuring magnitudes of the effects of aggregates and averages. It came to fascinate me much more.

I felt in a way that the thing which I am not prepared to do—I don't know of anybody else who can do this particular task. I rather hoped that what I'd done in capital theory would be continued by others. This was a new opening which was fascinating. The one situation would have meant working for a result which I already knew, but I had to prove it, which was very dull. The other thing was an open problem: What does economics really look like when you recognize it as the prototype of a new kind of science of complex phenomena, which could no longer employ the simple model of mechanics in physics, but had to deal with what then I described as "mere pattern predictions," certain limited predictions? That was so much more fascinating as an intellectual problem.

Q_6: Wouldn't you say in retrospect that capital theory in the Austrian sense ended with *Pure Theory of Capital?*

HAYEK: I'd say very largely. No one has done what I hoped would be done by others.

Q_6: At least the question of Keynesian aggregates is now being taken seriously, and you wound up as the man who fifty years ago first challenged it.

HAYEK: It is the disappointment with Keynes which has turned interest back to me. And the mere fact of unemployment combined with inflation at the same time suddenly disillusioned people.

Q_6: Some have argued that Keynes's *General Theory* was written purposely to confuse and to be complex. Do you think that's true?

HAYEK: Not as crass as this. He was so convinced that he was cleverer than all the other people that he thought his instinct told him what ought to be done, and he would invent a theory to convince people to do it. That was really his approach. While he was very untrained as an economist in economic history—you know he had a passion for Elizabethan era, for sixteenth century, was a great expert—but for the economic history of the nineteenth century, he was close to being ignorant, because he disliked it on aesthetic reasons. The nineteenth century is ugly.

Q_6: Why did he hate the nineteenth century so much?

HAYEK: Oh, because he believed Tawney and company on the history of labor. The impoverishment of the working class. It's all Dickens.

The only letter from Keynes that I have is what he wrote to me on *The Road to Serfdom,* which has been quoted again and again, where he sympathized very much with me and comes to the conclusion that there is a great danger, but in a country where people feel rightly we can avoid all these things.

The outbreak of war brought the removal of the LSE to Cambridge and the departure of most of my close colleagues to government service. For a time I was then the only senior economist of LSE, assisted only by two young men. But at least the lectures were a joint program with Cambridge, and for a while I gave the lectures on advanced economic theory for both institutions, while A. C. Pigou gave the elementary theory.

During the first year of the war we continued to live in London, and I went to Cambridge only for three days each week. But with the beginning of the bombing in September 1940, this became impracticable. As I could at first not get suitable accommodations at Cambridge, the Robbinses, who had then a cottage in the Chilterns, took my family for a year, while Keynes, with whom by that time I had become very friendly, got me rooms at King's College. In 1941 I finally succeeded in finding a house, or rather an adapted barn, in Malting Lane, where we lived until 1945.

Life at Cambridge during those war years was to me particularly congenial, and it completed the process of thorough absorption in English life which, from the beginning, I had found very easy. Somehow the whole mood and intellectual atmosphere of the country had at once proved extraordinarily attractive to me, and the conditions of a war in which all my sympathies were with the English greatly speeded up the process of becoming thoroughly at home—much more than in my native Austria from which I had already become somewhat estranged during the conditions of the 1920s. While neither on my early visit to the United States nor during my later stay there or still later in Germany did I feel that I really belonged there, English ways of life seemed so naturally to accord with all my instincts and dispositions that, if it had not been for very special circumstances, I should never have wished to leave the country again. And of all the forms of life, that at one of the colleges of the old universities—at least as it then was at Cambridge; Oxford I never knew well—still seems to me the most attractive. The evenings at the High Table and the Combinations Room at King's are among the pleasantest recollections of my life, and some of the older men I came then to know well, especially J. H. Clapham, remained, while they lived, dear friends.

PART THREE

A Parting in the Road

The light burden of teaching (there were very few students) and the short distances at Cambridge gave me more time for my own work than I ever had before. Though my main interest was still in pure economic theory, it was at Cambridge that I wrote *The Road to Serfdom*, developing certain ideas which I had already sketched in an article in 1938 and which had grown further as a result of those studies on the abuse and decline of reason to which I had devoted the first two years of the war and which I have mentioned earlier.

Q₁: *The Road to Serfdom* is the kind of book that the lay reader, it would seem to me, can deal with as opposed to a more technical economics book. The use of the word "foreigner" . . . in Britain is an interesting one. To what extent does—and I know you've done some recent thinking about this—culture, in some definition, play a role in the ordering of world activities?

HAYEK: There's something in that, but it is not necessarily the culture into which you are born that most appeals to you. Culturally, I feel my nationality now is British and not Austrian. It may be due to the fact that I have spent the decisive, most active parts of my life between the early 1930s and the early 1950s in Britain. But it was really from the first moment arriving there that I found myself for the first time in a moral atmosphere which was completely congenial to me and which I could absorb overnight.

I admit I had not the same experience when I first came to the United States ten years earlier. I found it most interesting and fascinating, but I did not become an American in the sense in which I became British. But I think this is an emotional affair. My temperament was more like that of the British than that of the Americans, or even of my native fellow Austrians. That, I think, is to some extent a question of your adaptability to a particular culture. At one time I used to speak fairly fluent Italian; I could never have become an Italian. But that was an emotional matter. I didn't have the kind of feelings which could make me an Italian; while at once I became in a sense British, because that was a natural attitude for me, which I discovered later. It was like stepping into a warm bath where the atmosphere is the same temperature as your body.

Q₁: What is it about you that makes you feel comfortable with the British?

HAYEK: The strength of certain social conventions which make people understand what your needs are at the moment without mentioning them.

Q₁: Can you give us an example?

HAYEK: The way you break off a conversation. You don't say, "Oh, I'm sorry; I'm in a hurry." You become slightly inattentive and evidently concerned with something else; you don't need a word. Your partner will break off the conversation because he realizes without your saying so that you really want to do something else. No word need to be said about it. That's in respect for the indirect indication that I don't want to continue at the moment.

Q₁: How would that differ in the United States? More direct?

HAYEK: Either he might force himself to listen too attentively, as if he were attentive, or he might just break off saying, "Oh, I beg your pardon, but I am in a hurry." That would never happen—I can't say never happen—but that is not the British way of doing it.

Q₁: How does it differ from the Austrian?

HAYEK: There would be an effusion of polite expressions explaining that you are frightfully sorry, but in the present moment you can't do it. You would talk at great length about it, while no word would be said about it in England at all.

* * *

Q₆: The sense of being at home in England must have helped you to master the nuances of the language.

HAYEK: During the war I played with *The Road to Serfdom* because it was the first time I felt I had come to master English, in the sense that I got enjoyment in writing in English. I mean, I had no difficulty in expressing technical arguments, but—

Q₆: You felt a real sense of mastery.

HAYEK: In fact you will find, if you take the trouble to read the beginning of the introduction and the first two or three chapters, that I really tried there to see how well I could write English, and I took great trouble, reading it out again and again, getting the swing of the thing.

Q₆: The rhythm, yes.

HAYEK: It would have taken me years to do it for the whole book. But stylistically, probably, part of the opening—the first two or three chapters and the introduction—was the best thing I have ever written. Really taking trouble and enjoying the awareness that at last I'd reached the stage where I could write English well, not only correctly, but good English. That went on all through the war, and gradually— I think I still have one or two versions of *The Road to Serfdom* on which I practiced. And I enjoyed doing it. I was perhaps a little tired of pure theory. These four years I spent on *The Pure Theory of Capital* were very hard years.

There's at least one other thing which is rather important, which you will get out of my texts. *The Counter-Revolution of Science* is a fragment of a very big book which I was then planning in a very different form. The intended title was *The Abuse and Decline of Reason*. And when I decided to write out *The Road to Serfdom*, it was really in anticipation of the argument of the decline of reason at the end. Much more popular than the original thing, because I was much too ambitious. The first time was meant to be the chapters which I have written on the Saint-Simoneans; Comte; the relation of Comte to Hegel; then there were two or three on France; then was to come one on Hegel and Marx. And I hated to turn to Marx. I had struggled with Marx in my student years. And I found it so depressing on turning to him, so I abandoned this idea of a long historical

account, and then came this systematic account of the decline of
reason. Nemesis and Hubris were titles.

*　*　*

Q₅: Was there not some confusion over *Road to Serfdom* as sort of
an observation of things that might be happening—

HAYEK: A very special situation arose in England, already in 1939,
that people were seriously believing that National Socialism was a
capitalist reaction against socialism. It's difficult to believe it now,
but the main exponent whom I came across was Lord Beveridge. He
was actually convinced that these National Socialists and capitalists
were reacting against socialism. So I wrote a memorandum for Beveridge on this subject, then turned it into a journal article, and then
used [my time during] the war to write out what was really a sort of
advance popular version of what I had imagined would be the great
book on the abuse and decline of reason. This was the second part,
the part on the decline of reason. It was adjusted to the moment
and wholly aimed at the British socialist intelligentsia, who all
seemed to have this idea that National Socialism was not socialism,
just something contemptible. So I was just trying to tell them,
"You're going the same way that they do."

   That the book was so differently received in America, and that it
attracted attention in America at all, was a completely unexpected
event. It was written so definitely in an English frame of reference—
and it was, of course, received in a completely different manner.
The English socialists, with few exceptions, accepted the book as
something written in good faith, raising problems they were willing
to consider. People like Lady Wootton wrote a very— In fact, with
her I had a very curious experience. She said, "You know, I wanted
to point out some of these problems you have pointed out, but now
that you have so exaggerated it I must turn against you!" In America
it was wholly different. Socialism was a new infection. The great enthusiasm about the New Deal was still at its height, and here there
were two groups: people who were enthusiastic about the book but
never read it—they just heard there was a book which supported
capitalism—and the American intelligentsia, who had just been bit-
ten by the collectivist bug and who felt that this was a betrayal of
the highest ideals which intellectuals ought to defend. So I was ex-
posed to incredible abuse, something I never experienced in Britain

at the time. It went so far as to completely discredit me professionally.

In the middle 1940s—I suppose I sound very conceited—I think I
was known as one of the two main disputing economists: there was
Keynes and there was I. Now, Keynes died and became a saint; and
I discredited myself by publishing *The Road to Serfdom*, which completely changed the situation.

The popular success of *The Road to Serfdom* was a complete
surprise to me. Though I long resisted the pull which threatened
to draw me from pure theory into more practical work, it had
ultimately a profound effect on my life. The immediate success
in England was no less surprising than that in the United States,
though it never took the spectacular form it did in the latter
country. I happened to experience the top of this curious boom,
since from March to May 1945, just when the book made the
best-seller list, I was on a lecture tour in the U.S., which was
one of the most curious experiences of my life.

The American publishers, the University of Chicago Press,
had originally arranged for a five-week visit, in the course of
which I should have repeated a series of three or four lectures
at five major universities in the East and Middle West. While I
was crossing the Atlantic in slow convoy (it was still during the
war) and without communications, the condensation of the book
in the *Reader's Digest* completely altered the position. I was suddenly if only temporarily famous, and on arrival was told that
the whole plan for my visit was changed, that I was to go on a
far-ranging popular lecture tour, and that all arrangements had
been put in the hands of a commercial lecture agency. So I,
who had never before done any popular lecturing to large audiences, found myself the day after my arrival lecturing—without
any preparation and on the subject I had not foreseen—to Town
Hall, New York, and discovering to my great surprise that I
could do it successfully.

The story of the whole tour, which took me as far west as
Oklahoma City and during part of which Chicago was my headquarters, is too long to tell here. But practically all my contacts
that led to later visits and finally made my move to Chicago
possible were made during this trip. I had in fact not been to
the U.S. since my visit as a graduate student twenty-one years

before, but then returned almost every year until I moved definitely at the end of 1949.

Q_6: Could you comment on the response to *The Road to Serfdom?*

HAYEK: In England *The Road to Serfdom* arrived at a stage where people had already become aware of the dangers of socialism. In America, I heard the new enthusiasm of all the New Dealers. And there was some violent reaction. I ought to say that the people who in England talked about it had read the book. In America it was discussed mostly by people who had not read it or, at most, read the condensation in *Reader's Digest.*

I believe I told you already that I did not get a penny from the *Reader's Digest* condensation, because University of Chicago Press had given it to the *Reader's Digest* free. And most people read it in that form. It was very, very well done, by Max Eastman; he did the condensation. Of course there are probably twelve times the number of people who have read it in the *Reader's Digest* form than read the complete book. It even reached at that time large numbers of people in prison or war camps. *Reader's Digest* was apparently distributed, particularly in the English camps, to prisoners of war. A number of Germans said, "I was learning English by reading the *Reader's Digest.*"

Anyhow, when I arrived in New York: "The original plan is off. You have suddenly become famous. You go on a lecture tour of the United States."

"I can't do that, I have never done any public lecturing."

"Well, that's all arranged, you must try and do it."

"When do we begin?"

"Oh, you are late already." It was a Saturday afternoon. "You start tomorrow morning at Town Hall in New York."

Meant nothing to me. What came to mind was this beautiful *New Yorker* cartoon [by Helen Hokinson] of a woman's club. I thought, Sunday morning, it can only be such a woman's club. When I was picked up at the Regency Hotel and taken downtown, I began to inquire from my chairman, who picked me up, "Well, what sort of audience do you expect?"

"The hall holds three thousand, but there's overflow."

"My God. I have never done such a thing. What am I supposed to lecture on."

"Oh, we have called the tune, 'Law and International Affairs.'"

"My God, I have never thought about it. I can't do this."

"Everything is announced, they are waiting for you."

So I was ushered into this enormous hall with all kinds of apparatus which are strange to me. At that time they had dictating machines, microphones, all completely new to me. My last recollection is, I asked the chairman, "Three-quarters of an hour?"

"Oh no, it must be exactly one hour, you are on the radio."

So I got up on a subject on which I had no idea, and I still know that I began with the sentence, "Ladies and gentlemen, I suppose you will all agree when I say—" I didn't know yet what I was going to say.

And then I discovered that American audiences are extremely grateful audiences, you can watch on their faces their interest—completely different from, say, an English audience; and gradually I worked them up into great excitement, and I got through this lecture with great success. I, who had never, literally, given a popular lecture, never lectured without a manuscript, suddenly found I was capable of popular lecturing of this kind.

I went all over the United States, as far as the mountains and back, and south, for five weeks, and gradually thought I had become quite an experienced public lecturer.

* * *

HAYEK: In the autumn of 1946, I believe, I managed for the first time to go to Germany to lecture for the British Council. I went both to English and American zones. My main quartering position was in Cologne, where I had, I think, my most moving experience as a university lecturer. I didn't have any idea the Germans knew anything about me, at that time; and I gave a lecture to an audience so crowded that the students couldn't get in, in an enormous lecture hall. And I discovered then that people were circulating hand-typed copies of *The Road to Serfdom* in German, although it hadn't been published in Germany yet.

Q6: What was the lecture itself on?

HAYEK: *The Road to Serfdom.* In addition to Cologne, I lectured in a few neighboring cities, including Darmstadt, which was particularly memorable because the place was laid absolutely flat by the war;

there didn't seem to be a city left, just great piles of rubble. I climbed through the rubble into an underground big hole to speak.

Q$_6$: Someone in London told me there was something called "the Gestapo speech," in which Attlee attacked you. Can you tell me anything about that?

HAYEK: The Gestapo speech was the speech by Churchill in which he—it must have been shortly after publication of *The Road to Serfdom*—where he was alleged later to have been inspired by *The Road to Serfdom*, and when he was predicting that a socialist government would lead to a Gestapo. And then Attlee accused Churchill in his reply that "Mr. Churchill was inspired by Friedrich August von Hayek."

Q$_6$: That's all there was to it?

HAYEK: That's all. When he was speaking, Churchill had the Gestapo all through it. This habit of socialists to call me "Friedrich August von Hayek" was not peculiar to Attlee; others had done the same thing. I was officially in socialist terms, "Friedrich August von Hayek."

Q$_6$: And there's a 1947 article about you in which you are described as Winston Churchill's economic advisor. There's nothing to that?

HAYEK: No. I met Churchill a single time.

Q$_6$: The headline reads: "Churchill Advisor Explains."

HAYEK: I happened to be dean of the faculty of economics and was invited to a dinner with Churchill before the conferring of a degree. During the dinner, I could see him swilling brandy in great quantities; and by the time I was introduced to him, he could hardly speak but at once identified me as the author of *The Road to Serfdom*. He was stock drunk. He said just one sentence: "You are completely right; but it will never happen in Britain." Half an hour later he made one of the most brilliant speeches I ever heard.

Q$_6$: Ernst Gombrich told me that he thought that the "Gestapo speech" may well have cost Churchill the election. Do you think there's anything to that?

HAYEK: I don't regard it as impossible. He was attacked by Attlee; and by Dalton, on that stage; in each case, with the allegation that he had got this from the Austrian economist Friedrich August von Hayek. In that connection, I became associated in the public mind with Churchill, but evidently he knew what the book contained. I knew that from the one encounter. I'm not even sure how far he has read—the whole thing?—and I never had any influence, any contact, beyond this one time. But this phrase of "a Gestapo" was in that speech used so much against him at the time, it may well be that that whole speech did more harm than anything else.

Q6: Another question I had was in the use of the word "von," as in "von Mises," "von Hayek," and so forth. I remember a story, which I can only vaguely recall, as to how Mises got his title, which as a Jew was rare, and it had something to do with his father's getting the title and inheriting it down. What were the details?

HAYEK: They were all inherited. First, the gentleman in the Mises story. The general story is, imagine that in England all the higher civil service were professional men and commercial people who get, through special merit, the title "sir," and inherit it to all their children. In Austria, instead of being called "sir," you are called "von," often from several generations back. Then there is the complication that this title was formally abolished and even prohibited with the Revolution of 1918, with the result that in Austria, slightly comically, nobody can legally use it of himself, but he is allowed to use it of another person. You are only prohibited from calling yourself "von" in Austria, but as a matter of politeness you will so address anybody who is historically entitled. This complication becomes even greater in my own personal case. I was a law-abiding citizen and completely stopped using the title "von," but it was of course inevitably on my birth certificate. So that when I got naturalized in England and for that purpose submitted the birth certificate, when I received the certificate of naturalization, my English name became suddenly "von Hayek." Now it was at a moment when I was very anxious to go on an English passport for a holiday to Europe, so instead of invoking the bureaucracy to change this, I put up with it. Ever since, officially, in Austria, I'm Mr. Hayek. But in England I'm officially Mr. von Hayek.

* * *

Q$_7$: Could you explain your intent in writing *The Road to Serfdom?*

HAYEK: It was aimed against what I would call classical socialism; aimed mainly at the nationalization or socialization of the means of production. Many of the contemporary socialist parties have at least ostensibly given up that and turned to a redistribution/fair-taxation idea—welfare—which is not directly applicable. I don't believe it alters the fundamental objection, because I believe this indirect control of the economic world ultimately leads to the same result, with a very much slower process. So when I was then talking about what seemed to be an imminent danger if you changed over to a centrally planned system, which was still the aim of most of the official socialist programs, that is not now of direct relevance. At least the process would be different. Some parts of the present welfare-state policies—the redistribution aspect of it—ultimately lead to the same result: destroying the market order and making it necessary, against the will of the present-day socialists, gradually to impose more and more central planning. It would lead to the same outcome. But my description of the process, and particularly the relative speed with which I assumed it would take place, of course, is no longer applicable to all of the socialist program.

Q$_7$: Away from reliance on central planning and toward using the budget for redistribution of income?

HAYEK: Exactly. I don't know whether I should say I flatter myself. I think socialism might have discredited itself sooner if it had stuck to its original program.

* * *

Editor's note: Reproduced in the following pages is a complete transcription of a radio broadcast of a discussion among Hayek and two University of Chicago professors in April 1945.

The Road to Serfdom

A Radio Discussion
The University of Chicago Round Table
in cooperation with the National Broadcasting Company
April 22, 1945

Around the Round Table . . .

Friedrich Hayek, professor of economics at the London School of Economics, was born in Vienna in 1899. He was educated at the University of Vienna, and in 1921 entered the Austrian civil service. He later became director of the Austrian Institute for Economic Research and served as a lecturer in economics at the University of Vienna. In 1931 he went to England to become a professor of economic science at the University of London, and since the middle 1930s he has been connected with the London School of Economics. He became a British citizen in 1938. He is the author of many books, among which are *Prices and Production* (1931); *Monetary Theory and the Trade Cycle* (1933); *Collectivist Economic Planning* (1935); *The Pure Theory of Capital* (1941); and *The Road to Serfdom* (1944).

Maynard C. Krueger, assistant professor of economics and member of the faculty of the College of the University of Chicago, studied both history and international politics before specializing in economics. He completed his undergraduate education at the University of Missouri in 1926. After receiving his A.M. from that institution in 1927, he joined the staff of Albion College as an instructor in history. He spent three years in Europe studying at the universities of Paris, Berlin, and Geneva. From 1928 until he joined the faculty of the University of Chicago in 1932, he taught in the School of Finance and Commerce at the University of Pennsylvania. He is now serving as national chairman of the Socialist party and in 1940 ran as vice-presidential candidate on the national Socialist ticket.

Charles E. Merriam, Morton D. Hull Distinguished Service Professor Emeritus of Political Science at the University of Chicago, was a member and served as vice-chairman of the National Resources Planning Board. He also was a member of the Commission on Recent Social Trends and of the President's Committee on Administrative Management. Professor Merriam has been active in Chicago politics, serving three terms as alderman in the City Council, and in 1911 was narrowly defeated for mayor of Chicago. He studied at Lenox College and the State University of Iowa, and received his A.M. and Ph.D. degrees from Columbia University. Professor Merriam has been a member of the political science department of the University of Chicago since 1900. He is the author of many books, among which are *A History of American Political Theories* (1903); *American Political Ideas, 1865–1917* (1921); *The American Party System* (1922); *New Aspects of Politics* (1925); *Political Power* (1934); *Role of Politics in Social Change* (1936); *The New Democracy and the New Despotism* (1939); *Prologue to Politics* (1939); *What*

Is Democracy? (1941); *On the Agenda of Democracy* (1941); and *Public and Private Government* (1944).

"The Road to Serfdom"

MR. KRUEGER: You just published a book, Professor Hayek, which is a general attack on socialists of all varieties, including the socialists of the Socialist party, of whom I am one. This discussion on today's Round Table is bound to be primarily a discussion of your main arguments. Would you restate for us in a word the essential thesis of your book?

MR. HAYEK: It is not really an attack upon socialists; it is rather an attempt to persuade socialists, to whom I have dedicated my book. My main thesis is that they are mistaken in the methods for getting what they want to achieve. There are two alternative methods of ordering social affairs—competition and government direction. I am opposed to government direction, but I want to make competition work.

MR. KRUEGER: This book is also an attack on planning. Professor Merriam, you are lecturing here right now on the relation between government and the economic order. How does the book impress you?

MR. MERRIAM: I have been engaged in planning, now, for some forty years—planning in Chicago, state planning, regional planning, national planning in Washington—and I have not found that our planning was leading toward serfdom but rather toward freedom, toward emancipation, and toward the higher levels of human personality. I find that this book is not particularly significant in our field except that it tends to confuse men in regard to the meaning of planning in this country.

MR. KRUEGER: I foresee some interesting discussion here and some controversy. Your main assertion, Hayek, is that planning leads to totalitarianism. Are there any qualifications you make to that statement?

MR. HAYEK: Surely, there are. In the way in which you use "planning" in this discussion, it is so vague as to be almost meaningless. You seem to call all government activity planning and assume that there are people who are against all government activity.

Mr. Merriam: In other words, you do not like the American use of the word "planning" and you are introducing another one?

Mr. Hayek: I do not know about the American use, and I still doubt whether it is a general use. It is your use.

Mr. Merriam: Across the street from here is the American Society of Planning Officials, with about twelve hundred members. There are hundreds of city planning boards and forty-eight state planning boards, and all kinds of planning has been going on in Washington for the last fifteen or twenty years. If you do not know that, I am reminding you of it now—and straight.

Mr. Hayek: I know that, but there are a good many people in America who oppose planning who do not mean by that opposition that they think that there ought not to be any government at all. They want to confine the government to certain functions. You know, I do agree that this discussion here, as elsewhere, has been very confused. What I was trying to point out is that there are two basic and alternative methods of ordering our affairs. There is, on the one hand, the method of relying upon competition, which, if it is to be made effective, requires a good deal of government activity directed toward making it effective and toward supplementing it where it cannot be made effective.

Mr. Merriam: I do not like to be brushed off so quickly on the American notion of planning. I read a comment only today of your book which said that "this will be an antidote to well-meaning and sentimental planners and socialists" without any discrimination whatsoever—anymore than you make any discrimination in your book.

Mr. Hayek: That I hope the book will be.

Mr. Merriam: It must be a disappointment, from this point of view, to have me, an American planner, tell you that we do not use your word in that sense and that we do not like the way in which you push it on us.

Mr. Krueger: Merriam, hold your horses for just a minute, and let us give this man a chance to explain to us and to our listeners the sense in which he is using this term "planning." You are not, I take it, refusing to allow public planning in all fields. Would you give us a bill of particulars of the sort of planning you are not attacking?

MR. HAYEK: There is the whole design of the legal framework within which competition works—the law of contract, the law of property, the general provisions to prevent fraud and deception. All these are entirely desirable activities, but let me more positively define planning against competition.

Whenever the government is asked to decide how much of a thing is to be produced, who is to be allowed to produce it, who is to be excluded from producing it, who is to have that privilege and this privilege—that is a kind of social system which is an alternative to the competitive system and which cannot be combined with it and which has been advocated for a hundred years at least by the great majority of socialists and which has gained great influence— I oppose it. It is against this kind of planning, exclusively, that I am arguing.

MR. KRUEGER: May we ask you some questions about that? What about limitation of working hours—a maximum-hours act? Is that compatible with your notions of proper planning?

MR. HAYEK: Yes, if it is not carried too far. It is one of these regulations which creates equal conditions throughout the system. But, of course, if it goes beyond the point where it accords with the general situation of the country, it may indeed interfere very much. If today you dictate that nobody is to work more than four hours, it may completely upset the competitive system.

MR. MERRIAM: Would any limitation on the hours of labor be objectionable in your judgment?

MR. HAYEK: Not "any," but they can be. There you have one of the instances where my objection is not one of principle but one of degree. It is one of the things which cannot be made to fit the question of the cost involved in that particular measure.

MR. KRUEGER: Is a minimum-wage law permissible?

MR. HAYEK: A general, flat minimum-wage law for all industry is permissible, but I do not think that it is a particularly wise method of achieving the end. I know much better methods of providing a minimum for everybody. But once you turn from laying down a general minimum for all industry to decreeing particular and different minima for different industries, then, of course, you make the price mechanism inoperative, because it is no longer the price mechanism which will guide people between industries and trades.

MR. MERRIAM: What about the TVA?

MR. HAYEK: There is a great deal of the TVA to which no economist in repute, and certainly not the laissez-faire people, will object. Flood control and building of dams are recognized functions of the government. I am under the impression that a good deal else has been tacked on to this scheme which need not have been done by public enterprise. But the principle of flood control and the like's being provided by the government is an entirely legitimate and a necessary function of the government.

MR. MERRIAM: Even if it involved a development of hydroelectric power, as the TVA does?

MR. HAYEK: That depends upon the circumstances. If the hydroelectric power really could not have been provided by private enterprise, I have no objection.

MR. MERRIAM: That is not a matter of logic but of practical adjustment.

MR. HAYEK: The whole question of whether you can or cannot create competitive conditions is a question of fact.

MR. MERRIAM: Not of logic?

MR. HAYEK: All I am arguing about is that, where you can create a competitive condition, you ought to rely upon competition.

MR. KRUEGER: Is a comprehensive system of social insurance a violation of your definition of good planning?

MR. HAYEK: Certainly not a system of social insurance as such, not even with the government helping to organize it. The only point where the problem can arise is how far to make it compulsory and how far, incidentally, it is used to strengthen the monopolistic actions of trade unions, because that is one way in which it may well eliminate competition.

MR. MERRIAM: You do not mean to say that you would be against any government social insurance, would you? You want to make it entirely optional?

MR. HAYEK: It might well be made optional, which is not in contra-diction to its being government-assisted, but why it needs to be made compulsory, I do not see in the least.

MR. KRUEGER: One of the reasons was that a great many people, the population at large, was supposed to get it. That was the reason for making it compulsory. I think that everybody is pretty well agreed on that.

MR. HAYEK: I do not know about that.

MR. KRUEGER: What do you think of a minimum guarantee of food, clothing, and shelter to people? Is that a violation of your definition of proper planning?

MR. HAYEK: What do you mean by "a minimum guarantee"? I have always said that I am in favor of a minimum income for every per-son in the country.

MR. MERRIAM: You used that in your own book. What did you mean by it?

MR. HAYEK: I will restate it in my way—I mean to secure a mini-mum income on which every one can fall back. You have it, of course, very largely in the form of unemployment insurance.

MR. MERRIAM: When Krueger used that term, you seemed disturbed.

MR. HAYEK: No, he turned it into a specific guarantee of particular things.

MR. KRUEGER: That was an exact quotation.

MR. MERRIAM: Of your book.

MR. KRUEGER: A minimum guarantee of food, clothing, and shelter. If that is permissible, then I am glad to hear you say so, because you do go considerably further than that. In the international field you want a power which can restrain the different nations from actions harmful to their neighbors. It seems to me that you do allow far more of public planning than most of the readers of your book in this country have assumed.

MR. HAYEK: I have noticed this, but I am not an anarchist. I do not suggest that a competitive system can work without an effectively enforced and intelligently drawn up legal system. Internally we have at least had an approach to it; internationally, we have not even had the legal system.

MR. KRUEGER: Could we ask you for a recitation of the sort of planning which would be proscribed in your ideal system? What kind of planning do you find objectionable?

MR. HAYEK: I have given you a general definition. It is any direct control of the volume or direction of production. If you want illustrations from this country, I think that I must give prewar illustrations. We could take the Agricultural Adjustment Administration, nearly all the NRA, or, more recently, the Guffey Coal Bill. There you have quite a long list.

MR. MERRIAM: Would you also include the tariff in there?

MR. HAYEK: Certainly all restrictions which prevent competition.

MR. MERRIAM: You would repeal all tariffs, would you?

MR. HAYEK: I am a convinced free-trader, and free trade is part of the same philosophy.

MR. MERRIAM: Without any limitations or qualifications whatsoever?

MR. HAYEK: One thing which makes me unhappy is that so many people who take up my book are not free-traders and do not see that this is an essential part of the same philosophy.

MR. MERRIAM: Are you against price parity for the farmer?

MR. HAYEK: If "price parity" means that a particular price is to be insured by the government, I certainly am, because it means the price system of competition is completely ineffective.

MR. MERRIAM: You think, then, that if we are to avoid the road to serfdom, we must repeal all tariffs and the price parity for the farmers?

MR. HAYEK: It would be one of the most certain means to avoid that path.

MR. KRUEGER: Another thing in which I am interested is the problem of planning with regard to unemployment. You explain in your book why people want more planning now than the last generation

wanted, and you do so without ever using the word "unemployment," which comes into your book very, very rarely. What kind of
planning is justifiable in tackling the unemployment problem?

MR. HAYEK: Essentially, what is required and likely to be effective, I
believe is largely—almost exclusively—in the field of monetary policy, although I do not agree with many of the current ideas. I mean
the fact that the government has important functions in providing
conditions which will lead to a high and stable level of employment, nobody can doubt. Whether particular measures are effective
or not is a very technical question.

MR. MERRIAM: Is the Federal Reserve Bank on the road to serfdom?

MR. HAYEK: They make mistakes.

MR. MERRIAM: In principle, I mean?

MR. HAYEK: No. That the monetary system must be under central
control has never, to my mind, been denied by any sensible person.
It is part of that framework within which competition can work.

MR. MERRIAM: You did not hear the debate on the adoption of the
Federal Reserve Bank Board bill.

MR. HAYEK: I have studied the history of the Federal Reserve System
in very great detail.

MR. MERRIAM: You did not hear it denounced, then, as socialistic in
character?

MR. HAYEK: Do not make me responsible for all the nonsense which
has ever been talked about by anybody.

MR. MERRIAM: The words which you do not like you call nonsense
or vague.

MR. HAYEK: You regard it as nonsense.

MR. MERRIAM: I regard it as nonsense, yes, but, as a realist, I look at
what is happening in this country—I mean in America—as distinguished from Austria or the Continent or England.

MR. KRUEGER: A statement which seems to me to be nonsense is one
of the major assertions of your book. That is the statement made in
very plain language that it is historically true that the rise of totalitari-

anism and specifically fascism was not a reaction against collectivist trends in Europe but was the inevitable consequence of the trend toward socialism. That seems to be to me such a clear perversion of the historical fact that I would like to hear it restated in some terms which I could understand.

Mr. Merriam: In limited terms.

Mr. Hayek: It is my main conviction and the main thesis of the book. What it comes to, simply, is that the trend toward socialism was the main cause in putting greater and greater powers, over all activities, in the hands of the government. In Europe, once governments directly controlled a large part of the social activity, they had to tell the people in the service of what ends these activities had to be employed. Thus they had to shift from the control, merely, of our material activity to the control of our ideals and beliefs.

Mr. Merriam: In answer to which I must say that, starting in Germany in 1899 as a student at the University of Berlin and having been there many, many times—particularly along a period of 1924, 1926, 1929, 1930, and 1932—I have exactly the opposite impression. It was not the fact of communism but the fear of communism that was the most powerful factor in the development of Naziism.

Mr. Krueger: If we cannot agree upon the historical observation concerning the relationship between collectivism and socialism and fascism, let us turn to the logical argument. Your argument, Hayek, is that central planning must necessarily lead to totalitarianism. I would like to explore that idea further.

Mr. Merriam: What do you mean by "central planning"? I am a little bit confused on that part.

Mr. Krueger: That is the first thing I would like to consider. I would like to consider with the two of you whether that can be done by definition—for example, simply defining planning as totalitarian—or whether there is a real logic to this, because I was not able to follow the logic in the book.

Mr. Hayek: I used the term "central planning" in exactly the same sense in which all the people in the past have suggested that we could make things much better if we took them out of the hands of free enterprise and entrusted them to government control. That is how I used this term. Once you do this, a thing happens which these people did not foresee, but which is a necessary consequence of this. Because the government takes control of the means, it also has to decide for what ends they are being used.

MR. MERRIAM: The original Marxians were anarchists, were they not? They did not believe in the state at all.

MR. HAYEK: They hoped that ultimately the state would be abolished, but they proposed a route which went through the omnipotence of the state and merely promised the abolition of the state in a very distant future and never explained how it was to come about.

MR. MERRIAM: That is still a doctrine, however, is it not?

MR. HAYEK: There are so many Marxian schools.

MR. MERRIAM: Can we not say that Lenin ought to be accepted as a prophet of communism?

MR. HAYEK: I doubt whether anyone in communist Russia believes that the state will ever disappear.

MR. MERRIAM: We are dealing with the logic of the situation and not the practical facts. That is the doctrine, is it not?

MR. KRUEGER: You wind up, Hayek, using the term "socialism," the terms "communism," "totalitarianism," "planning," and "collectivism" interchangeably from one paragraph to the other. You substitute the one for the other, which leads us to inquire what you do really mean by planning. You insist, for example, that it requires control of the individual's activities.

That is, that if there is going to be economic planning, a central planning authority must decide on people's occupational choice, abolish freedom of occupational choice, must decide on exactly what commodities and services people are going to consume as specific people, and in what quantity, and must proceed, further, to establish control over the individual's thinking and speaking, and even over his family relations. You suggest all this in your book. What is there about central planning which requires this control over individual activities?

MR. MERRIAM: When you say "central planning," you are excluding my kind of planning.

MR. KRUEGER: He is also excluding my kind of planning.

MR. MERRIAM: Washington is central planning, from one point of view, or the National Planning Association, sitting in Washington, composed of private aids.

MR. HAYEK: I do not use these terms interchangeably, Krueger. I say that collectivism is a method which can be used for many different things and that the others are various specimens of collectivism. But I say that certain results follow from the method and not from the ends which people mean to achieve. That method of central planning which is proposed as an alternative method of organizing production to take the place of competition means that a government, or some central authority, must take complete control of the resources.

MR. MERRIAM: But if "central planning" does not mean that, then, of course, it does not mean that as within the United States.

MR. HAYEK: I have defined and used the term, I believe, consistently in this meaning, and I believe that there is a good deal of this kind of central planning even in the United States.

MR. MERRIAM: I challenge that. Would you enumerate some of those?

MR. HAYEK: I have given you a list before.

MR. MERRIAM: You mean the AAA; but they are constitutional anyway. They are not leading us on the road to serfdom; they are dead.

MR. HAYEK: Most of the war controls are central planning, but it is only temporary.

MR. MERRIAM: You expect the war to be conducted by precincts and counties? War has to be centralized, does it not?

MR. HAYEK: During the war, we all have to go to some extent totalitarian.

MR. MERRIAM: You have no objection to that, do you?

MR. HAYEK: No, because you might sacrifice for a time part of your freedom to preserve it in the long run.

MR. KRUEGER: As against this definition of planning which, by defini-

tion, requires control of all the individual's activity, I would like to
suggest to you that there has been a great deal written, which you
must undoubtedly have read, in exposition of a democratic kind of
planning based upon decentralization and based upon the use of
rules rather than upon the use of discretionary authority in the making of decisions and based upon the maintenance of the democratic
political process as the essential control over government officials
by the people. But you seem to ignore all that. You insist, for example, that planning is incompatible with the rule of law.

Merriam, you are a rule-of-law man. What do you say about this?

MR. MERRIAM: I know something about the rule of law, yes, but it
seems to me that the great gap in Hayek's studies, among many
gaps, is that he does not reckon with public administration and with
management. He regards anything that is delegated to an administrator or a manager as being irrational, if I understand him correctly.

MR. HAYEK: There are so many points. Krueger, yours is, I believe,
the most important.

MR. MERRIAM: I regard mine as the most important.

MR. HAYEK: I must begin with Krueger. These new experiments of
some of you socialists to design an alternative to what used to be
the traditional method of socialism is intellectually most fascinating.
They are, in fact, the result of some recognition of the very dangers
I point out. I do not think that you have gone at all far enough. You
do not see how great the danger is. You are not yet avoiding it with
the modifications you propose, but you, at least, have seen the beginning of it.

But my point is that I have been arguing about the kind of socialism which determines our present development, not about the kind
of speculative socialism which is altogether about five years old and
which has been discussed in about a dozen articles and learned
journals in which the authors are very doubtful that it will ever become a practical issue.

MR. MERRIAM: What is it you are discussing? I seem to be a little mys-
tified. Krueger, do you know or understand what he is talking
about?

MR. KRUEGER: I think that he is simply dismissing everything that has been very intelligently written on the question of how planning can be operated democratically, because he insists upon a definition by which planning is undemocratic.

MR. MERRIAM: He is pushing us out of the picture. By definition his definition is a definition, I am sure.

MR. HAYEK: I used the definition which, up to about five or ten years ago, all socialists I knew used and all socialists asserted could be put into effect under the democratic system. Now you and I have come to the conclusion that all their old conceptions of government-directed economy could not be achieved in a democratic system. I draw the conclusion that it applies to all socialism. You, in reaction, have now designed a new type of socialism which you think avoids it, and I am watching these experiments with the greatest interest.

MR. MERRIAM: I do not see how you can be sure, then, that you cannot have democratic conditions under a system which you say has never been tried yet.

MR. HAYEK: You may have entirely different controls. I am all in favor of development and experiment.

MR. MERRIAM: I think that we have more faith in democracy than you do. I would say so from certain passages in your book.

MR. KRUEGER: Let me push that point a little bit further. You insist, Hayek, that any kind of planning is incompatible with the rule of law, and you dismiss in one small footnote anything that has been written on socialist planning of a democratic nature or character. You seem to place no faith whatsoever in the political process as a means of keeping government responsible to the people. Is that really your position? Do you have no faith in the political process as a means of establishing responsibility?

MR. HAYEK: If you use central planning in the sense in which I use it—government direction of production—I am quite convinced that it cannot be effectively controlled by the democratic process. It requires a degree of agreement among the people which we can never expect in a free society. It requires methods by which people are meant to agree; otherwise you will never get your democratic checks.

MR. MERRIAM: In your chapter on "Why the Worst Get on Top," you seem to express grave doubts about the ability of a democratic society to accomplish very much. You say, for example, that the more intelligent people are, the less likely they are to agree. If that is so, the value of our educational process is lost.

MR. HAYEK: I am saying that people like you, Merriam, are inclined to burden democracy with tasks which it cannot achieve and, therefore, are likely to destroy democracy.

MR. MERRIAM: You think that that is my view. My point is that that is the making of democracy and that the weakness of democracy is caused by the fact that people listen to what some people think is your judgment.

MR. HAYEK: That is where we differ.

MR. KRUEGER: Hayek, I am as skeptical as you are about the all-powerful state.

MR. MERRIAM: What do you mean by the "all-powerful" state?

MR. KRUEGER: I am talking in his terms. He has used the words "all," "comprehensive," and so on in every chapter.

MR. MERRIAM: No state is all-powerful.

MR. KRUEGER: I do not want to be saved from the private concentrations of economic power of the nineteenth century by the development of a totalitarian state, but if you were seriously interested in that, Hayek, it seems to me you would be interested in the improvement of the political process by which you establish a connection between people and their government. Instead of that you say, and I will quote: "The periodical election of representatives to which the moral choice of the individual tends to be more and more reduced is not an occasion on which his moral values are tested." It seems to me that, unless this political process can be made the occasion for moral values, you are going to be in great trouble.

MR. HAYEK: If you take the sentence out of its context, it is very misleading.

MR. KRUEGER: I suggest that each of us make a final statement to clarify for our listeners our essential position on this subject.

A Parting in the Road

MR. MERRIAM: I find that the modern trend is toward freedom— freedom in far richer measure than ever before in human history. Serfdom and slavery are behind us, not before. War and unemployment—the great curses of mankind—are in the process of abolition by human, democratic effort which brings together in joint enterprise, both public and private, the creative forces of government, business, labor, agriculture, and the church.

MR. KRUEGER: If you define planning in such a way that it has to be totalitarian, then there is no way you can make it democratic; but planning is compatible with maintaining procedural rules which limit discretionary power. Liberty and equality and security can all be combined, but some freedoms, I think, have to be abolished or limited in order to do that. One of them is the freedom to own privately and to control for profit the means of life which are essential to others. Instead of restricting morality to the individual's conduct as its proper field, moral principle has to get into the political process and to operate through political programs and political parties. Otherwise liberty is simply going to be a word in "Liberty League."

MR. HAYEK: I am not shaken by what you are saying. You see, you are still talking about an old controversy—about whether the state ought to act or ought not to act at all. The whole effort of my book was to substitute a new distinction for the older silly and vague idea. I had realized that some kind of state action is extremely dangerous. Therefore, my whole effort was to distinguish between legitimate and illegitimate action. I have attempted to do that by saying that, so far as the government plans for competition or steps in where competition cannot possibly do the job, there is no objection; but I believe that all the other forms of government activity are highly dangerous.

PART FOUR

Chicago–Freiburg

The longest of my postwar visits to the United States before 1949 was the one in the spring and early summer of 1946, when I spent in succession two months each at the University of Chicago and Stanford University. It was during that period, when I had more free time than I had had for many years, that I seriously resumed work on the psychological ideas I had begun more than twenty-five years before and which were ultimately published in *The Sensory Order*.

After my visit [on the lecture tour in 1945], the financial temptation to do more semi-popular writing and lecturing was considerable, and some of my friends strongly urged me to stay and reap the possible harvest. Offers of various kinds were not wanting. But I felt neither attracted by this task nor thought that I had the skill to do it easily. Indeed I felt that this sort of popular lecturing and writing had a corrupting effect on one's mind and that in the long run I would do more for the political ideals I cared for if I stuck to strictly academic activities. But that I had for once exercised some practical influence and at the same time earned a fair amount of extra money made me feel entitled to take a complete holiday from practical concerns and to devote my energies for a while to wholly abstract problems. I probably also felt it as a smart that some of my more leftish acquaintances (with considerable cheek) gave me to understand that in their opinion I had ceased to be a scientist and had become a propagandist. At any rate, I decided that I would reward myself for what seemed to me a duty performed by completely disregarding for a time what was expected of me and doing exclusively what happened to interest me most at the moment. These were my old ideas on theoretical psychology, which had been revived by the work on the methodology of the social sciences I had done during the early years of the war.

I should never have wished to leave England, certainly not if I could have continued to live at Cambridge, [even though] I did begin to feel the atmosphere of a highly specialized institution like LSE somewhat narrow and the work there—because of the long distances to travel and the evening teaching—increasingly exhausting. What made me accept the offer from Chicago [in 1950] was in the first instance solely that it offered the financial possibility of that divorce and remarriage which I had long desired and which the war had forced me to postpone for many years. In fact the post at the Committee on Social Thought at the University of Chicago offered me almost ideal opportunities for the pursuit of the new interests I was gradually developing. As professor of social and moral science, I was allowed there to devote myself to almost any subject I cared and to do as much or as little teaching as I wanted. I had, as a matter of fact, become somewhat stale as an economist and felt much out of sympathy with the direction in which economics was developing. Though I had still regarded the work I had done during the 1940s on scientific method, the history of ideas, and political theory as temporary excursions into another field, I found it difficult to return to systematic teaching of economic theory and felt it rather as a release that I was not forced to do so by my teaching duties.

Q₆: Didn't the Volker Fund have something to do with your move to the U.S. [in 1950]?

HAYEK: On one of these [1945] lecture tours—the whole reason I tell this story—one of the most significant of these lectures was at the Economic Club in Detroit. I had my headquarters then at the Quadrangle Club of the University of Chicago, since it was the University of Chicago Press that was behind it, and the whole thing was in the hands of the national concerts and artists organization. That lecture in Detroit was quite successful, and next morning, or day after, back in Chicago, a certain gentleman turned up at my club and said, "Professor, I'm not going to take much of your time, but a book like *The Road to Serfdom* ought to be written for the United States. Can you do it?"

"I know nothing."

"Can it be done?"

"Well, I suppose, if you choose a suitable man, it can be done."

"How much would it cost?"

"I am not very familiar with American prices, but I suppose something like $10,000 a year [$60,000 in current prices] for three years, and it could be done."

"Money is yours."

That was Mr. Luhnow. I didn't take him very seriously. But I had some long discussions about this with Henry Simons, who had become my great friend in Chicago, and there were some complications, but finally I had to return to England. Had to report to Luhnow in the course of the journey that I couldn't do anything about it.

His cable back: "Will you come back on your terms to do it?"

"Not in your pay. If you arrange for a university to invite me to come as a visiting professor, I might incidentally look after this."

"Which universities would you prefer?"

All by cable, you know. I said, "Chicago," where I started talking with Henry Simons, and then I mentioned that I had not yet been to the West Coast; I mentioned Stanford as a possibility. Within three weeks I had invitations from the chancellors of three universities. Arrangements were made to divide a semester between Chicago and Stanford.

Q6: What became of the project to produce an American *Road to Serfdom?*

HAYEK: I had nearly persuaded Henry Simons to take the post on condition that Aaron Director, who was then working in Washington, come to join him and work with him.

Q6: This would have been at Chicago? And Director was the brother-in-law of Milton Friedman?

HAYEK: Yes. He used to be in Chicago, had taken a wartime job in Washington, and was in Washington at the time, while Henry Simons was the one with whom I negotiated. Now the thing broke off with first Aaron refusing to take this job helping Henry Simons. And then a curious event happened. After I had moved on to Stanford to make further efforts there, Henry Simons died quite suddenly. Anyhow, as a result of this, Aaron Director felt the obligation to continue as a dear friend what he hadn't been willing to do earlier with Henry Simons. So Aaron Director went with this Volker money to Chicago with the official mission to write a "Road to Serfdom" for the United States, which he never did. This was my beginning with Luhnow. I had after this no further direct contact with him except attending some of the discussion meetings which he called, but I have reason to suspect that when a little later John Nef began to make attempts to persuade Hutchins to call me to Chicago, he was instrumental. I was proposed first to the faculty of economics, but they turned me down.

. . . Whoever was behind wanting me there was persistent and shifted his efforts from the faculty of economics to the Committee on Social Thought. Which to me ultimately was much more attractive, because after teaching economic theory for twenty years I was a little tired, and the invitations from the Committee on Social Thought indicated that I could lecture on any borderline subject in the social sciences and, if at any time I didn't want to teach, it would not be required. This, with a correspondingly higher salary, was irresistible. So I did go to Chicago.

The chapters on the history of ideas contained in *The Counter-Revolution of Science*, that is, the essays on the Saint Simonians and Comte written in London in 1940, are the most ambitious attempt in a field which has long interested me. To it belong the various biographical sketches of economists (Gossen, Wieser, Cantillon, Menger and particularly Henry Thornton, my favorite among these essays) that I have written at various times. But the work on the Saint Simonians in particular led unexpectedly to my devoting a great deal of time to John Stuart Mill, who in fact never particularly appealed to me, though I achieved unintentionally the reputation of being one of the foremost experts on him. This came about through my noticing in tracing Saint-Simonian influence on England how much of the important correspondence of John Stuart Mill which threw light on this issue was either available only widely dispersed among many publications, often in places difficult to find, or only in manuscript.

A survey of the available unpublished correspondence then revealed such a wealth of material of this kind—and among it the peculiarly fascinating correspondence of Mill with his later wife—that I was tempted into starting a systematic collection and even publication of the most interesting material. The accident that I came across this material at a period of the war when I had both time to spare and a suitable and otherwise unemployable assistant (Dr. Bosch) available tempted me to go much deeper with the project than I had intended. But after publishing the correspondence between John Stuart Mill and Harriet Taylor [1951] and putting all my material at the disposal of Mill's successful biographer, Michael Packe, I unloaded all my accumulation of transcripts of Mill letters on Dr. Francis Mineka of Cornell University who, I am sure, will do the job of editing much better than I could have done.

My work on Mill bore one unforeseen but very pleasant fruit. In editing the correspondence with his wife, I had had to omit most of the long letters Mill had written to her from the long journey to Italy and Greece he had taken for reasons of health in the winter and spring of 1854–55. It occurred to me that it might be interesting to repeat the journey after exactly a hundred years with the aim of producing a fully annotated edition of the letters. I succeeded in persuading the Guggenheim Foundation to give me a substantial grant to finance the journey, and thus my wife and I were able to spend a delightful seven months travelling by car, first through the west and south of France, through Italy as far south as Naples, and then around most of Sicily, to Corfu and Athens, which provided the center from which we visited Euboea, Delphi, and much of the Peloponnesus. Since we were able to travel by car so much more quickly than Mill had been able to travel once he got beyond the railways, and though we tried in general to be at the different places at the dates when Mill had visited them, we saved enough time to make from Naples a side trip to Egypt to deliver the lectures on "The Political Ideal of the Rule of Law," which I had been invited by the Bank of Egypt to give.

These lectures, together with the constant preoccupation with Mill's thinking, brought it about that after our return to Chicago in the autumn of 1955, the plan for *The Constitution of Liberty* suddenly stood clearly before my mind. There is a story connected with it, however, which I like to tell. In his *Autobiography*, Mill describes how the conception for his book *On Liberty* came to him walking up the steps of the capitol at Rome. When I repeated this on the appropriate day a hundred years later, no inspiration, however, came to me. And as I later noticed, it was indeed not to be expected, since Mill had fibbed: The letters show that the idea of writing such a book had come to him before he reached Rome. Nevertheless, shortly after the conclusion of our journey, I had before me a clear plan for a book on liberty arranged round the Cairo lectures. In the three succeeding years, I wrote drafts of each of the three parts of *The Constitution of Liberty*, revising the whole during the winter of 1958–59, so that I was able to take the finished manuscript to my American publishers on my sixtieth birthday, May 8, 1959. (The production of the book was completed in December 1959, but the official publication date was given as February 9, 1960.)

Soon after the appearance of *The Constitution of Liberty* in May 1960, I began to suffer a severe depression which lasted exactly a year. I then ascribed it to an effect of my cessation of smoking (because of a false alarm caused by my dentist discovering a sore spot on my palate), and it did indeed almost instantaneously disappear when after a year I returned to my pipe. But I am now more inclined to regard it as an early attack of the same sort of depression from which I am now [March 1972] suffering for almost two years [a depression that persisted until some time before the award of the Nobel prize in 1974]. That first attack ended while we were spending part of the spring of 1961 at the University of Virginia in Charlottesville, a visit most of which was overshadowed by that depression.

I am increasingly inclined to believe that my miserable state in the early 1970s was chiefly due—after some initial heart disturbance in 1969—to my personally very nice and well-regarded Salzburg doctor treating me erroneously for diabetes and giving me a medicine that produced too low a sugar content of my blood, that was the main cause of that "inner trembling," as I called the state, which intellectually disabled me. I have since learnt that this description I had invented is familiar to doctors as a symptom of too low a sugar content in the blood. What speaks for this explanation is that even after ceasing to take that medicine, my sugar level has remained on the low side, which is, I believe, very unlikely in a person tending to diabetes, although it could possibly have been due to the reduction of my weight from around 89 kg to not much above 70 kg.

Much as I enjoyed the intellectual environment that the University of Chicago offered, I never came to feel as much at home in the United States as I had done in England. I also was much concerned about the inadequate provision for my and my wife's old age which that position offered me: a lump sum at a comparatively early retirement age (65). When I received in the winter of 1961–62 an unexpected offer of a professorship at the University of Freiburg im Breisgau, which not only was to run three years longer but also secured at least for me a moderate pension for life, I could have no hesitation in accepting the offer and have never regretted the move. The eight years we spent there were in many ways very satisfactory. I had, once again, to become an economist, but was able to concentrate in my teaching on the problems of economic policy, on which I felt I still had something of importance to say. We were very fortunate in finding an attractive apartment and particularly enjoyed the beautiful environment of the Black Forest.

I also was fortunate to preserve almost to the end of that period at Freiburg my full energy and health and working capacity. And though after my seventieth birthday my powers began noticeably to decline—and I have still not completed the work on which I was engaged during most of these years—they were on the whole very fruitful years. We also travelled during these years more than ever before: four visits to Japan (with side trips to Taiwan and Indonesia), and finally, as a return trip from a five-month stay at the University of California at Los Angeles, a flight through the South Pacific (Tahiti, Fiji, New Caledonia, Sydney, and Ceylon).

Soon after settling down at Freiburg, I started work on what grew into the project of a rather ambitious book on law, legislation, and liberty [*Law, Legislation and Liberty*, in 3 vols., 1973–79], intended as a kind of supplement to *The Constitution of*

Liberty. Most of what I published during the Freiburg period are offshoots of that work, and when we left Freiburg after eight years, I had completed (except for a concluding chapter) an excessively long manuscript, which I still believe contains some important ideas but which, in its present form, seems to me unsuitable for publication.

Q₅: I remember you telling me once about a project. As I remember it, it was to get the backing of the Ford Foundation to reestablish the University of Vienna—it was in the 1950s.

HAYEK: Well, to reestablish its tradition. My idea was to create something like an institute of advanced studies, and to bring all the refugees who were still active back to Vienna—people like Schrödinger and Popper and— Oh, I had a marvelous list! I think we could have made an excellent center, if the thing could have been financed. But what grew out of it is the present Ford Institute at Vienna, which is devoted entirely to mathematics, economics, and statistics, which I don't particularly approve of. I think the plan miscarried, not least because the University of Vienna did not display great enthusiasm for such a scheme.

One of the chief benefits I derived from the success of *The Road to Serfdom* was that through the various lecture tours to which it led or by correspondence, I was brought into contact with a larger number of men who held similar ideas on the issues raised in the book than I had thought existed. I found that not only in the United States but also in several countries on the Continent there existed individuals or small groups who still preserved the great liberal tradition but, in trying to restate and defend it, felt as isolated as our little group at the London School of Economics, where not only my closest friend Lionel Robbins but also several other colleagues—Arnold Plant, Frank Paish, and Frederic Benham—were in essential accord with my views.

I found that I derived so much instruction by the discussion with similarly minded men in other places—such as Henry Simons and his Chicago group, Wilhelm Röpke at Geneva, and a German group led by Walter Eucken—that the wish grew in me to bring these men together as an international group for a discussion of the problem which their efforts to revive the liberal tradition raised. I felt that only within a group which shared the same basic philosophy was a fruitful discussion of these problems possible, and that we had much to learn from each other since each had pushed his efforts of developing the underlying ideals in a different direction, which in many other respects most of us had inevitably accepted some of the fashionable current ideas which were really incompatible with the liberal principles.

But though in the years immediately following the war I thought and talked a good deal about this idea, it would probably have remained a dream if I had not in Switzerland met a very able organizer who put my plan into execution. A certain Dr. Albert Hunold at Zurich had raised some funds to enable Röpke to start a liberal quarterly, but some frictions which had arisen between them made this plan impracticable. Dr. Hunold, however, obtained the consent both of the donors and of Röpke to use the money already collected in Switzerland to finance the conference which I proposed. When I succeeded in obtaining some additional funds from an American admirer of *The Road to Serfdom*, it became possible to arrange such a conference in the spring of 1947, of which I was able to determine both the membership and the program, while all the labor of organization was performed by Dr. Hunold. The ten-day conference at Mont Pèlerin above Vevey on the Lake of Geneva comprised some thirty-six scholars and publicists from the U.S., England, and several Continental countries, and proved such a success that it was resolved to turn it into a permanent association, which derived its name from the place of its first meeting.

For the next twelve years—during which I acted as president of the society and during which it grew rapidly in membership—I was able to arrange with the help of Dr. Hunold meetings in different locations almost every year, to which I owe many friends and many new ideas. But the worldly ambitions which Dr. Hunold developed, on whom I had relied for all organizational work, ultimately made collaboration impossible, and I found it necessary to insist that we both resign to make room for a new leadership. Younger members took the initiative, and, after a critical period of a year or two, the society resumed its programs and is still, after nearly twenty-five years, flourishing—though they are now, in 1971, after a period during

which its ideals seemed to be advancing in the world, again
threatened by a new trend to collectivism.

I have often envied men whose knowledge is theirs, stored in
an orderly and easily reproducible manner, and who are able at
any time not only to restate chains of reasoning that they have
once learnt or themselves worked out but to do so almost in the
words in which they first became acquainted with them. They
are the men with the ready answers, the effective teachers, and
I believe also the good writers: The latter requires that one
oversee one's subject as a whole and be constantly aware at what
point in the larger pattern of reasoning he stands at the moment.

But I am not sure whether the men of this type, whose memory gives them a ready command of their knowledge, are also
as likely to make original contributions as those whose mind
does not move so easily in the established grooves. I, at any
rate, am sure that I owe most of the original ideas I have ever
had to the fact that I did *not* have the conventional answers to
the well-known questions ready, that I had painfully to work
them out anew almost every time, and that in that process I
often discovered the flaws or inadequacies of the generally held
views.

In comparing my own capacities and methods of work with
those of colleagues and friends, I became increasingly aware of
the existence of two very different mental types, of which I
represent a fairly pronounced instance of one. They differ
chiefly in the role which precise memory or easy reproduction
of chains of argument plays in one's intellectual make-up. My
capacity for reproducing from memory a segment I have read or
heard is very small indeed. Even as a young man, though I
had a fairly good short-term memory, and while an argument I
followed or even a story I heard would leave permanent effects
on my thinking, I would rarely be able to restate it. It was as if
they at once became part of a composite photograph, a contribution to my conception of the world, but not an account of the
world I could again use as such.

What original ideas I have had actually did not come out of
an orderly process of reasoning. I have always regarded myself
as a living refutation of the contention that all thinking takes
place in words or generally in language. I am as certain as I

can be that I have often been aware of having the answer to a problem—of "seeing" it before me, long before I could express it in words. Indeed, a sort of visual imagination, of symbolic abstract patterns rather than representational pictures, probably played a bigger role in my mental processes than words. I believe that the strongly visual type of memory and the lack of a verbal memory are often connected.

I have always been attracted by the idea of composite photographs (that is, the result of photographs of several different faces being superimposed upon each other), which were fashionable before my time and of which I perhaps never saw an instance. But they seem to represent a characteristic feature of my mind—I do not remember an argument, but somehow absorb part of it into what I already know. It would be a very great effort to appropriate an argument so that I could reproduce it, perhaps easiest on a subject on which I know nothing at all, but almost impossible on a question on which I have thought myself. But even in studying a new subject, the result of reading through the first textbook would be rather blurred and indistinct. And I used to prefer not to work through the same textbook again but rather to read another one on the same subject. Gradually things would fall into their places, and while I would have acquired the gain of working out in my own mind an answer to most relevant questions, I would not have a clear conspectus of the whole ready in my mind or be able to give twice the same exposition of a topic.

About the time of my move to Cambridge, and particularly in the new company of the High Table of King's College, I became rather depressed by my decreasing capacity closely to follow English conversations. It was only after the war, when I again visited German-speaking countries, that I discovered that it was not my understanding of English but my hearing that was deteriorating greatly. I had long been deaf on the left ear (as I thought as a consequence of the explosion of a shell in the war, but the doctors said that it is the effect of an infection in childhood), but until above forty my hearing on the other ear was sharp enough to make up for it. It has since increasingly deprived me of the enjoyment of society and almost completely of the theater, which at one time had been one of my regular pastimes.

Though it has not yet become as bad as I at one time feared, it is in a large measure responsible for my appearing much more unsociable than I actually am.

It was also during the Cambridge years that I could indulge most in my hobby of collecting old books on economics. I had started this already at Vienna, and at first in connection with the book I was then planning on the history of monetary theory and policy, a special collection I sold in 1939 to the Bank for International Settlements at Basle to raise the down payment for the house I then bought. Visits to Oxford, Cambridge, and Edinburgh, and a few other places in the provinces offered in the 1930s still ample opportunities to acquire nineteenth- and eighteenth-century works; and though I could no longer try to emulate the great collectors of earlier generations, I believe that the collection I ultimately built up (and in 1969 sold to the University of Salzburg) was as good as any which colleagues of my generation were still able to bring together. I added to it continuously through purchases from catalogues until after the war, when their source practically dried up (or at least became impossibly expensive), and once succeeded in better balancing the at first chiefly English collection by buying from the widow of my slightly older Viennese colleague Ewald Schams a good collection of French eighteenth-century economic literature.

Apart from such sports as mountaineering and skiing and, in my early years in Austria, family history, I have unfortunately developed no other hobbies which now, in my old age, I very much regret.

Q6: Wasn't mountaineering more than just a hobby for you?

HAYEK: Perhaps in furthering my understanding of the English intellectual atmosphere of the nineteenth century. It was the same sort of combination of intellectual work and mountaineering which fitted so well, such as Leslie Stephen's book on mountaineering. In my case, mountaineering was connected with botany. I knew the English mountaineering literature, and that helped me to fit into the English atmosphere.

Q6: Didn't mountaineering become your connection with the economist Pigou?

HAYEK: We were both at Cambridge during the war. He taught the elementary economics course, and I did the advanced one. But it was only when I looked at a certain book by Richard Deacon, which is a pseudonym, that it occurred to me why Pigou suddenly got interested in me. Deacon suggests that Pigou was interested in people who could cross frontiers. I had forgotten about the fact that in 1939 I wanted to visit Austria, and I didn't want to be suspected of having any special privileges with the Germans. In fact, I was visiting my present wife. Very soon after that, Pigou got interested in me, and the contrast of his sudden interest in me and then suddenly dropping me—after he had asked me to come up to the Lake District and stay with him, and climb with him—fits in so perfectly with the Deacon story. But as late as July or August of 1939, I went to Austria very much in the awareness that I could risk it, even though it was likely that war might break out at any moment. I knew those mountains so well that I could just walk out.

Q_6: Your plan was to go over the mountains in Carinthia?

HAYEK: I knew the land well enough, even better than the Vorarlberg-Switzerland boundary. The mountains in the west, the Swiss, are recent glacier mountains, where it might be a little difficult to go by oneself. I had many friends in that region.

Though I have become as purely a scholar as can be conceived and today should not wish another form of life, it was not what I was expecting or thought would best suit me. It has been to a large extent the external circumstances of living in foreign countries—and most of the time as an alien less familiar with everyday life than most of my fellows—which kept me from all practical participation in public life, and even as a scholar drove me from the more concrete and empirical to the more abstract aspects of scientific work, where alone I could hope to have an advantage over my fellows. Had I remained in my native country, or even had I continued in England after I had become completely assimilated (an effect produced mainly by experiencing the war in England, with all my sympathies on her side), I should almost certainly have been drawn into public and political activities or administrative work. The latter I did not really care for, though my belief that I was no good at it was not entirely true. When the necessity arose, I believe I at least competently performed my duties.

I have often been acutely aware of the fact that—I believe, more than most other people—my thought was directed wholly to the future. I seem very early to have lost the capacity quietly to enjoy the present, and what made life interesting to me were my plans for the future—satisfaction consisted largely in having done what I had planned to do, and mortification mainly that I had not carried out my plans. As I was not overambitious and did not overestimate my capacities, I usually succeeded, and was during most of my life fairly content, at least so long as I had any definite tasks to do.

Q$_5$: You wrote a book in psychology, too; I remember that book [*The Sensory Order*].

HAYEK: I still believe this is one of my more important contributions to knowledge. And, curiously enough, the psychologists are now discovering it.

Q$_5$: Yes, I have seen some references within the last year or so.

HAYEK: It's now twenty-five years old, and the idea is fifty-odd years old.

Q$_5$: Could you perhaps summarize that notion?

HAYEK: I think the thing which is really important about it, and which I could not do when I first conceived the idea, is to formulate the problem I try to answer rather than the answer I want to get. And that problem is, What determines the difference between the different sensory qualities? The attempt was to reduce it to a system of causal connections, or associations, you might say, in which the quality of a particular sensation—the attribute of blue, or whatever it is—is really its position in a system of potential connections leading up to actions.

You could, in theory, reproduce a sort of map of how one stimulus evokes other stimuli and then further stimuli, which can, in principle, reproduce all the mental processes. I say "in principle" because it's much too complicated ever to do it. It led me, incidentally, to this distinction between an explanation of principle and an explanation of detail—pattern prediction, as I now know it—

which I really developed in my psychological work and then applied to economics.

Q₅: Yes, I think pattern prediction is a very important concept that most economists still sort of miss.

HAYEK: It's the whole question of the theory of how far can we explain complex phenomena where we do not really have the power of precise prediction. We don't know of any laws, but our whole knowledge is the knowledge of a pattern, essentially.

* * *

Q₆: Did you not once mention Schrödinger in connection with *The Sensory Order*?

HAYEK: To my great surprise, he was the one man who seemed to have fully understood *The Sensory Order*. But of course he was working on just this sort of problem. I had known Schrödinger when he was a *Gymnasiast*. His father was an amateur botanist as well as an industrialist. He was a member of my father's circle, who regularly met at our house. Sometimes young Schrödinger came along; he was about five or six years my senior. Then of course he moved to London.

* * *

Q₆: I see you as a man in the intellectual tradition of Kant and the Kantian movement. Mises also said that he was—the language indicates that he was—and yet the two of you disagreed on epistemology. That's the thing that has baffled me. You're both Kantians in perspective, yet you call him a utilitarian. How would you distinguish the two traditions?

HAYEK: It is again a complex story. You know the book by John Gray about me [*Hayek on Liberty*, 1984]. Of course he interprets me as a Kantian. I first was inclined to say, "You exaggerate the influence. I've never studied Kant very carefully." But the fact is that at the crucial age of, say, twenty or twenty-one, I got very fascinated by the works of a Kantian contemporary named Alois Riehl, who wrote a great work on criticism and two semi-popular introductions. I suppose what I know about Kantian philosophy comes largely from a Kantian. So I first told Gray, no, I knew far too little of Kant directly to justify this, then I had to admit that indirectly I got a good deal.

Q$_6$: You are not a utilitarian in your perspective.

HAYEK: Certainly not now. To begin with, I think it was Mises himself who made me familiar with utilitarianism, and in my early stages I studied them very much. In fact so much, that I discovered in studying the papers of Jeremy Bentham at University College that Bentham had been a very good economist, who had done very noticeable work on monetary theory.

At that time I had started on the highly urgent work of organizing the Bentham papers, which were an awful mess. That broke down when the first Bentham committee at University College, which I had started, broke up during the war, and the definite start of an edition was made only after I'd left London. If I'd still been in London, I have no doubt University College would have asked me to come in again and to resume the thing, but I had by then gone to America. I had nothing to do with the great Bentham edition, and I've since become fairly skeptical, because I had become so very much aware that Bentham had been influenced much more by the French eighteenth-century tradition than by the English, or I should say Scottish—

Q$_6$: The Scottish rationalists.

HAYEK: I had discovered the Scots and found that the real root of my ideas lay with Ferguson and these people, and there was a very distinct conflict between that tradition and the Benthamite tradition. And then my many years of work on John Stuart Mill actually shook my admiration for someone I had thought a great figure indeed, with the result that my present opinion of John Stuart Mill is a very critical one indeed.

* * *

Q$_6$: Can you say something about your contention that the theory of evolution emerged from the humanities?

HAYEK: The model which made the idea of evolution generally known in the beginning of the nineteenth century was Sir William Jones's discovery of the connections of the Indo-European languages. By that time everybody was aware of the process of evolution in society.

Q₆: I've not heard that example before. I know that linguistics dates from that time, but I had not thought of it in that connection.

HAYEK: There were linguists, contemporaries of Darwin's, who said, "Oh, we have been Darwinians long before Darwin." But I don't think this illustration has ever been given. But clearly you have a full account of the evolution of varied types from one original type.

Q₆: Did anyone ever challenge Jones on the grounds of the Tower of Babel or Biblical authority?

HAYEK: I don't think theologians were concerned. Nothing like the theological position against Darwin.

* * *

HAYEK: I'm becoming a Burkean Whig.

Q₆: That's quite a combination.

HAYEK: I just assume—I think Burke was fundamentally a Whig; and I think Adam Smith was. Curiously enough, Mrs. Thatcher—I'm sure I've never told her yet. The last time I met her she used the phrase, "I know you want me to become a Whig; no, I am a Tory." So she has felt this very clearly.

* * *

Q₂: You have written an extraordinarily difficult book on capital theory [The Pure Theory of Capital, 1948]—in my opinion, it's difficult. What message did you want to convey in that book?

HAYEK: To put it briefly, I think it's that while Böhm-Bawerk was fundamentally right, his exposition in terms of an average period of production was so oversimplified as to mislead in the application. And that if we want to think the Böhm-Bawerk idea through, we have to introduce much more complex assumptions. Once you do this, the things become so damned complicated it's almost impossible to follow it.

Q₂: Did you have any idea the work was going to be that complicated when you undertook it?

HAYEK: No, no. I certainly didn't. It very gradually dawned upon me that the whole thing seemed to change its aspect once you could not put it in the simple form that you could substitute a simple average period of production for the range of investment periods. The average period of production is the first model showing a principle, but it is almost inapplicable to the real situation. Of course, the capital that exists has never been built up consistently on the basis of a given set of expectations but by constantly reusing accumulated real capital assets for new purposes that were not foreseen. So the dynamic process looks very different.

I think the most useful conclusions drawn from what I did are really in Lachmann's book on capital. Like so many things, I am afraid, which I have attempted in economics, this capital-theory work more shows a barrier to how far we can get in efficient explanation than sets forth precise explanations. All these things I've stressed—the complexity of the phenomena in general, the unknown character of the data, and so on—really much more point out limits to our possible knowledge than our contributions that make specific predictions possible.

This is, incidentally, another reason why my views have become unpopular: A conception of scientific method became prevalent during this period which values all scientific fields on the basis of the specific predictions to which they would lead. Now, it was pointed out that the specific predictions which economics could make were very limited and that at most you could achieve what I sometimes called pattern predictions, or predictions of the principle. This seemed to the people who were used to the simplicity of physics or chemistry very disappointing and almost not science. The aim of science, in that view, was specific prediction, preferably mathematically testable, and it was pointed out that when you applied this principle to complex phenomena, you couldn't achieve this. This seemed to people almost to deny that science was possible. Of course, my real aim was that the possible aims of science must be much more limited once we've passed from the science of simple phenomena to the science of complex phenomena. And people bitterly resented that I would call physics a science of simple phenomena, which is partly a misunderstanding, because the theory of physics ends in terms of very simple equations. But that the active phenomena to which you have to apply it may be extremely complex is a different matter. The models of physical theory are very simple indeed.

So far as the field of probability, that's another part. But it is this intermediate field, which we have in the social sciences, where the elements which have to be taken into account are neither few enough that you can know them all nor a sufficiently large number that you can substitute probabilities for the new information. The intermediate-phenomena field is a difficult one. That's a field with which we have to deal both in biology and the social sciences. And they're complex. They become, I believe, an absolute barrier to the specificity of predictions that we can arrive at. Until people learn themselves that they can't achieve these ends, they will insist on trying. They will think that somebody who does not believe this specificity can be achieved is just old-fashioned and doesn't understand modern science.

Q_2: John Hicks wrote about you, and I want to quote this: "When the definitive history of economic analysis during the 1930s comes to be written, a leading character in the drama—it was quite a drama—will be Professor Hayek. There was a time when the new theories of Hayek were the rivals of the new theories of Keynes." Why do you think your theories lost out to the theories of Keynes?

HAYEK: There are two sides to it. One is, while Keynes was disputed as long as he was alive—very much so—after his death he was raised to sainthood. Partly because Keynes himself was very willing to change his opinions, his pupils developed an orthodoxy: you were either allowed to belong to the orthodoxy or not.

At about the same time, I discredited myself with most of my fellow economists by writing The Road to Serfdom, which is disliked so much. So not only did my theoretical influence decline, most of the departments came to dislike me, so much so that I can feel it to the present day. Economists very largely tend to treat me as an outsider, somebody who has discredited himself by writing a book like The Road to Serfdom, which has now become political science altogether.

Recently—and Hicks is probably the most outstanding symptom—there has been a revival of interest in my sort of problems, but I had a period of twenty years in which I bitterly regretted having once mentioned to my wife after Keynes's death that now Keynes was dead, I was probably the best-known economist living. But ten days later it was probably no longer true. At that very moment, Keynes became the great figure, and I was gradually forgotten as an economist.

Part of the justification, you know, was that I did only incidental
work in economics after that. I guess there is one more aspect. I
never sympathized with either macroeconomics or econometrics.
They became the great fashion during the period, thanks to Keynes's
influence. In the case of macroeconomics, it's clear. But Keynes himself did not think very highly of econometrics, rather to the contrary.
Yet somehow his stress on aggregates, on aggregate income, aggregate demand, encouraged work in both macroeconomics and
econometrics. So, very much against his own wishes, he became
the spiritual father of this development towards the mathematical
econometric economics. Now, I had always expressed my doubts
about this, and that didn't make me very popular among the reign-
ing generation of economists. I was just thought to be old-fashioned,
with no sympathy for modern ideas, that sort of thing.

* * *

Q₆: Do you think the Chicago school were influenced by your being at Chicago?

HAYEK: Simons I should have had a great hope for, and his death
was a catastrophe. The others are in a methodological line; they are
in effect macroeconomists and not microeconomists. Stigler least of
all; Friedman very much. And this is a continual problem for me.
Milton and I agree on almost everything except monetary policy. In
this sense, the old group who saw this ethic derive from Wesley
Clair Mitchell's creation of the Institute of National Economic Research [National Bureau of Economic Research], led by Arthur
Burns—another personal friend of mine with whom I do not agree
on economics—and they are in effect logical positivists, methodo-
logically. They believe economic phenomena can be explained as
macrophenomena, that you can ascertain cause and effects from aggregates and averages. But although in a sense it seems to be true,
there is no necessary connection. In fact I should have preferred to
demonstrate historically that every period of inflation ends with a
crash. But the historical demonstration is no proof that this must be
so. The reason why it happens cannot be accounted for by macroeconomic analysis.

Now that, Milton Friedman just pooh-poohs. Stigler, if you can
discuss it with him, he will see the problem. The other, one of the
most gifted men in the Chicago School, is Gary Becker, and he is

also theoretically a more sophisticated thinker. But Friedman has this magnificent expository power. He is on most things, general market problems, sound. I want him on my side. You know, one of the things I often have publicly said is that one of the things I most regret is not having returned to a criticism of Keynes's treatise, but it is as much true of not having criticized Milton's [*Essays in*] *Positive Economics,* which in a way is quite as dangerous a book.

* * *

Q₂: Have the economic events since you wrote on trade-cycle theory tended to strengthen or weaken your ideas on the Austrian theory of the trade cycle?

HAYEK: On the whole, strengthen, although I see more clearly that there's a very general schema which has to be filled in in detail. The particular form I gave it was connected with the mechanism of the gold standard, which allowed a credit expansion up to a point and then made a certain reversal possible. I always knew that in principle there was no definite time limit for the period for which you could stimulate expansion by rapidly accelerating inflation. But I just took it for granted that there was a built-in stop in the form of the gold standard, and in that I was a little mistaken in my diagnosis of the postwar development. I knew the boom would break down, but I didn't give it as long as it actually lasted. That you could maintain an inflationary boom for something like twenty years, I did not anticipate.

While on the one hand, immediately after the war I never believed, as most of my friends did, in an impending depression, I anticipated an inflationary boom. My expectation was that the inflationary boom would last five or six years, as the historical ones had done, forgetting that then the termination was due to the gold standard. If you had no gold standard—if you could continue inflating for much longer—it was very difficult to predict how long it would last. Of course, it has lasted very much longer than I expected. The end result was the same.

Q₂: The Austrian theory of the cycle depends very heavily on business expectations being wrong. Now, what basis do you feel an economist has for asserting that expectations regarding the future will generally be wrong?

HAYEK: I think the general fact that booms have always appeared with a great increase of investment, a large part of which proved to be erroneous. That, of course, fits in with the idea that a supply of capital was made apparent which wasn't actually existing. The whole combination of a stimulus to invest on a large scale followed by a period of acute scarcity of capital fits into this idea that there has been a misdirection due to monetary influences, and that general schema, I still believe, is correct.

But this is capable of a great many modifications, particularly in connection with where the additional money goes. You see, that's another point where I thought too much in what was true under pre-war conditions, when all credit expansion, or nearly all, went into private investment, into a combination of industrial capital. Since then, so much of the credit expansion has gone to where government directed it that the misdirection may no longer be overinvestment in industrial capital but may take any number of forms. You must really study it separately for each particular phase and situation. The typical trade cycle no longer exists, I believe. But you get very similar phenomena with all kinds of modifications.

Q₂: You've already talked a little bit about your involvement with the socialist calculation debate. What effects do you feel the debate had on the theory of socialism?

HAYEK: Of course, it had some immediate effects. When Mises started it, there was still the idea very prevalent that there was no need for calculation in terms of value at all. Then came the idea that you could substitute values by mathematical calculation; then there came the idea of the possibility of socialist competition. All these were gradually repressed. But as I now see, the reason why Mises did not fully succeed is his very use of the term 'calculation.' People just didn't see why calculation should be necessary.

I mean, when I now look at the discussion at that time, and Mises asserts that calculation is impossible, I can [understand] the reply: Why should we calculate? We have the technical data. We know what we want. So why calculation at all? If Mises, instead of saying simply that without a market, calculation is impossible, had claimed that without a market, people would not know what to produce, how much to produce, and in what manner to produce, people might have understood him. But he never put it like this. He assumed everyone would understand him, but apparently people didn't.

Q₂: To what extent do you think the debate has slowed down the spread of national economic planning in the Western world?

HAYEK: Well, it's reviving again. It had died down very much, but when two years ago [1976] in the U.S. this planning bill of Senator Humphrey's and the agitation of Leontief and these people came forward, I was amazed that people were again swallowing what I thought had been definitely refuted. Of course, Leontief still believes firmly in it. I don't think he ever understood any economics, but that's a different matter.

Q₂: To what extent do you think that general-equilibrium analysis has contributed to the belief that national economic planning is possible?

HAYEK: It certainly has. To what extent is very difficult to say. Of the direct significance of equilibrium analysis to the explanation of the events we observe, I never had any doubt. I thought it was a very useful concept to explain a type of order towards which the process of economics tends without ever reaching it. I'm now trying to formulate some concept of economics as a stream instead of an equilibrating force, as we ought, quite literally, to think in terms of the factors that determine the movement of the flow of water in a very irregular bed. That would give us a much better conception of what it does.

But ultimately, of course, it goes back to the assumption of what the economists pleonastically call 'given data,' this ridiculous concept that, if you assume the fiction that you know all the facts, the conclusion you derive from this assumption can apply directly to the world. My whole thinking on this started with my old friend Freddy Benham joking about economists speaking about given data just to reassure themselves that what was given was really given. That led me, in part, to ask to whom were the data really given. To us, it was of course [given] to nobody. The economist assumes [the data] are given to him, but that's a fiction. In fact, there's no one who knows all the data or the whole process, and that's what led me, in the thirties, to the idea that the whole problem was the utilization of information dispersed among thousands of people and not possessed by anyone. Once you see it that way, it's clear that the concept of equilibrium helps you in no way to plan, because you could plan only if you knew all the facts known to all people; but since you can't possibly know them, the whole thing is vain and a misconception partly inspired by this concept that there are definite data which are known to anyone.

Q_2: Do you feel that mathematics has an important role to play in economic theory?

HAYEK: Yes, but algebraic mathematics and not quantitative mathematics. Algebra and mathematics are a beautiful way of describing certain patterns, quite irrespective of magnitudes. There's one great mathematician who once said, "The essence of mathematics is the making of patterns," but the mathematical economists usually understand so little mathematics that they believe strong mathematics must be quantitative and numerical. The moment you turn to accept this belief, I think the thing becomes very misleading—misleading, at least, so far as it concerns general theory. I don't deny that statistics are very useful in informing about the current state of affairs, but I don't think statistical information has anything to contribute to the theoretical explanation of the process.

Q_2: What is your assessment of game theory?

HAYEK: I don't want to be unkind to my old friend, the late Oskar Morgenstern, but while I think his book is a great mathematical achievement, the first chapter which deals with economics is just wrong. I don't think that game theory has really made an important contribution to economics, but it's a very interesting mathematical discipline.

*   *   *

Q_7: How far would you like to see the developments of the last thirty years reversed? What kind of society would you envisage that could evolve from the present starting point?

HAYEK: I would still aim at completely eliminating all direct interference with the market—that all governmental services be clearly done outside the market, including all provision of a minimum floor for people who cannot make an adequate income in the market. [It would then not be] some attempt to control the market process but would be just providing outside the market a flat minimum for everybody. This, of course, means in effect eliminating completely the so-cial justice aspect of it, that is, the deliberate redistribution beyond securing a constant minimum for everybody who cannot earn more than that minimum in the market. All the other services of a welfare state are more a matter of degree, how they are organized. I don't object to government rendering quite a number of services; I do ob-ject to government having any monopoly in any case. As long as only the government can provide them, all right, but there should be a possibility for others trying to do so.

Q_7: You do not object, then, to government's production of ser-vices, for example, if private production is not precluded?

HAYEK: Yes. Of course there is one great difficulty. If government does it—supplies it below cost—there's no chance for private com-petition to come in. I would like to force government, as far as it sells the services, to do so at cost.

Q_7: Even if it is involved in also financing the demand. You say that you would allow a government to provide a minimum, a floor; are you then also thinking of special, particular functions—health care, for example—or are you thinking simply in terms of an income floor?

HAYEK: Simply in terms of an income. From what I've seen of the British National Health Service, my doubt and skepticism has rather been increased. No doubt that in the short run it provides services to people who otherwise would not have got it, but that it impedes the progress of medical services—that there, as much as anywhere else, competition is an essential condition of progress—I have no doubt. And it's particularly bad, because while most people in Brit-ain dislike it, everybody agrees it can never be reversed.

Q_7: But the essential point is whether competition is provided or not, not whether the government is in this line of activities.

HAYEK: Exactly. But you know I now extend it even to money.

Q_7: Yes. I was going to bring that up. You returned recently to your early interest in monetary theory. Let me ask, first, why you have come to focus on money again recently. It was an interest of yours through some time in the 1930s.

HAYEK: It was a difference between me and nearly all my friends, who were in favor of flexible exchanges, and my support of fixed exchange rates, which I had intellectually to justify. I was driven to the conclusion that I wanted fixed exchange rates, not because I was convinced that it was necessarily a better system but [because] it was the only discipline on governments which existed. If you released the governments from that discipline, the democratic process—which I have been analyzing in different conditions—was bound to drive it into inflation. Even my defense of fixed exchange rates was, in a way, limited. I was against abandoning them only where people wanted flexible exchanges in order to make inflation easier.

When the problem arose in Germany and Switzerland, when it was a question of protecting them against imported inflation, I was myself supporting [flexible exchanges]. In fact, I argued in Germany that Germany kept too long fixed exchange rates and was forced to inflate by them, which they ought not to have done. It was confirmed to me by the people of the German *Bundesbank* that they were aware of this, but they still had the hope that the system of fixed exchange rates would restrain the inflation [in the United States] from doing even more inflation, and that they brought deliberately the sacrifice of swallowing part of the inflation in order to prevent it from becoming too large in the rest of the world.

That was very much my point of view. But that led me, of course, to the question of whether this was the best discipline on monetary policy, and to the realization that what I'd taken for granted—that the discipline of the gold standard was probably the only politically practicable discipline on government—could never be restored. Even a nominal restoration of the gold standard would not be effective because you could never get a government now to obey the rules of the gold standard.

These two things forced me [to the conclusion]—and I first made the suggestion as a bitter joke—that so long as governments pursue policies as they do now, there will be no choice but to take the control of money from them. But that led me into this fascinating problem of what would happen if money were provided competitively. It opened a completely new chapter in monetary theory, and discovering there was still so much to be investigated made the subject never again very interesting to me. I still hope—the two editions of the pamphlet on denationalizing money were done, incidentally, while I was working on my main book—to do a systematic book

which I shall call *Good Money*. Beginning really with what would
be good money—what do we really want money to be—and then
going on to the question of how far would the competitive issue of
money provide good money in terms of that standard.

Q_7: Would you agree that the most important step in this direction
would have less to do with who issues money than simply separat-
ing the so-called unit of account, in which private parties make con-
tracts, from the government-issued money, to get around, in effect,
legal-tender provisions and so on?

HAYEK: Yes, in a way. You know, I started remarking against the
idea of a common European currency, saying why not simply admit
all the other currencies competing with yours, and then you don't
need a standard currency. People will choose the one which is best.
That, of course, led me to the extension: Why confine it to other
government monies and not let private enterprise supply the money?

Q_7: But there's a question that extends to other aspects of your
work—to *Law, Legislation and Liberty* as well—that I would like to
raise here, which bothers me and I think some other people as well.
The process whereby the Western countries gave up first the gold
standard, and then what you call a discipline—and I agree there is
a discipline—of fixed exchange rates: Is that not an evolutionary
process, and are you not, with these proposals, in effect rationally
trying to reconstruct, rationally trying to controvert, as it were, a process of evolution?

HAYEK: No, it's a process of evolution only within the limits set by
the powers of government. Even within control there is still an evolutionary process, but so many choices are excluded by governmental
powers that it's not really a process which tries out all possibilities
but a process which is limited to a very few possibilities that are per-
mitted by existing law.

Q_7: But you have referred to the development of democratic government into omnipotent government, and certainly the trend has been
in that direction. Is that not a process of social evolution?

HAYEK: Again, it's an inevitable consequence of giving a government unlimited powers, which excludes experimentation with other
forms. A deliberate decision by a man has put us on a one-way

track, and the alternative evolutions have been excluded. In a sense, of course, all monopolistic government limits the possibilities of evolution. I think it does it least if it confines itself to the enforcement of general rules of conduct, but I would even go so far as to say that even very good world government might be a calamity because it would preclude the possibility of trying alternative methods. I'm thoroughly opposed to a world government.

Q$_7$: Of any form?

HAYEK: Any form.

Q$_7$: So to the question of what mistakes of evolution may be corrected by, as it were, rationalist intervention, you would answer by saying, well, there are certain processes of development where the course taken by the actual development has been dictated by—

HAYEK: —the use of force to exclude others.

Q$_7$: Yes. Are those the only instances in which you would interfere with spontaneous changes in social structure?

HAYEK: It depends on what you mean by interfere. They are the only cases in which I would admit intervention in the sense of experimenting with an alternative without excluding what is actually happening. I think there may even be a case for government coming in as a competitor, as it were, with other developments. My objection is that government assumes a monopoly and the right to exclude other possibilities.

Q$_7$: So in certain sectors, for example, where we are dissatisfied with the private outcome, you would—

HAYEK: —let the government try and compete with private enterprise.

*   *   *

Q$_6$: What prompted your return to the psychological ideas of *The Sensory Order*?

HAYEK: After *The Road to Serfdom*, I felt that I had so discredited myself professionally, I didn't want to give offense again. I wanted to be accepted in the scientific community. To do something purely scientific and independent of my economic view. I thought I could do it in a summer term and turn it into a decent English exposition, but of course it took well over three years.

Q_6: But *The Sensory Order* is not really independent of your economic views; it ties them together.

HAYEK: Of course. One sees this in retrospect rather than while one is doing it. I must say that the insights I gained—and I can't say now when—both from the first stage in 1920 or later in the 1940s, were probably the most exciting events that ever occurred to me, which shaped my thinking. But it works both ways. What I'd done in economics helped me to do this biological work as much as the opposite.

* * *

HAYEK: You have made me think about the past. I hesitate, because it sounds a little like self-praise, but it isn't, it's self-discovery. In a sense I am fearless, physically, I mean. It's not courage. It is just that I have never really been afraid. I noticed it in the war. It is common among young people that they are so fearless that they get into danger, but I never really had any fear of death, and that is connected with a certain stability. I am also a stranger to the sort of dizziness which one experiences in heights.

Q_6: You must have been fearless to go on those airplane expeditions in the great war where you were acting as an artillery spotter.

HAYEK: Excitement, in a sense; but not a matter of fear. Once the Italians practically caught us. One in front, firing through the propeller. When they started firing, my pilot, a Czech, spiralled down. I unbelted myself, climbed on the rail. My pilot succeeded in correcting the spin just above the ground. It was exciting.

Q_6: I would have been terrified.

HAYEK: You might put it differently. I lack nerves. I believe this is a thing that I inherited from my mother. She was like that.

Q_6: As well as the iron aunt that you told me about. May I take up another tack? You write in one of your books about Menger's problem, accounting for the rise of institutions without intention. I wonder whether there is anything that one can call Hayek's problem? Something that stayed all the way through, or developed.

HAYEK: The formation of complex orders. And recognition.

Q6: When did that begin as a problem for you?

HAYEK: It is so difficult to say when I became aware. When I did my studies on the methods of the sciences, I was struck by the complexity and the matters of degree, and it is not so difficult to apply the same principles. I suppose the decisive moment, you can probably trace it, was when I reached the idea of "explanation of the principle."

Q6: That is in *The Sensory Order,* and it is also in your article "Degrees of Explanation," which you wrote for the *British Journal for the Philosophy of Science* [1955]. There is a wonderful convergence thoughout your work of many different strands coming together. Did you have in the early 1920s a leading problem that you can identify?

HAYEK: What I had in mind in early years was a purely practical concern, wanting to find my way about, not yet fully aware that to do this I needed a theory. I was in search of a theory but didn't know yet what a theory really was.

* * *

Q3: A fellow Austrian great, the late Joseph Schumpeter, wrote *Capitalism, Socialism and Democracy* in 1942. In that book, Schumpeter predicted the collapse of capitalism due, not to its weakness (as Marx had predicted), but due to its strengths. Specifically, the tremendous economic abundance that would flower from the capitalist seed would produce an age of bureaucrats and administrators, displacing the innovators and entrepreneurs that had made it all possible. This, in turn, would undermine the social fabric upon which capitalism rested: a widespread acceptance and respect of private property. How does Schumpeter's thesis concerning the inherent political instability of capitalism fit in with your own theories on our road to serfdom?

HAYEK: There is some similarity in the nature of the prediction. But Schumpeter was really enjoying a paradox. He wanted to shock people by saying that capitalism was certainly much better but it will not be allowed to last, while socialism is very bad but it is bound to come. That was the sort of paradox he just loved.

Underlying this is the idea that certain trends of opinion—which he correctly observed—were irreversible. Although he claimed the opposite, he had, in the last resort, really no belief in the power of argument. He took it for granted that the state of affairs *forces* people to think in a particular manner.

This is fundamentally false. There is no simple understanding of what makes it necessary for people under certain conditions to believe certain things. The evolution of ideas has its own laws and depends very largely on developments which we cannot predict. I mean, I'm trying to move opinion in a certain direction, but I wouldn't dare to predict what direction it will really move. I'm hoping that I can just divert it moderately. But Schumpeter's attitude was one of complete despair and disillusionment over the power of reason.

Q₃: Are you optimistic about the future of freedom?

HAYEK: Yes. A qualified optimism. I think there is an intellectual reversion on the way, and there is a good chance it may come in time before the movement in the opposite direction becomes irreversible. I am more optimistic than I was twenty years ago, when nearly all the leaders of opinion wanted to move in the socialist direction. This has particularly changed in the younger generation. So, if the change comes in time, there still is hope.

PUBLICATIONS AND LETTERS
MENTIONED IN TEXT

Boring, Edwin G. Review of *The Sensory Order* in *Scientific Monthly* (March 1953).

Carnap, Rudolf. Letter to Karl Popper. In the Popper-Hayek correspondence in the archive of the Hoover Institution, Stanford, California. (First referred to by Hayek in the preface to the 1976 edition of *The Road to Serfdom.*)

Catchings, Waddill, and William Trufant Foster. *Money*. Boston and New York: Houghton Mifflin, 1923.

Friedman, Milton. *Essays in Positive Economics*. Chicago and London: Univ. of Chicago Press, 1953.

Galbraith, John Kenneth. *A Life in Our Times*. Boston: Houghton Mifflin, 1981.

Hayek, F. A., ed. *Collectivist Economic Planning*. London: George Routledge & Sons, 1935. Hayek's contribution reprinted as chapters 7 and 8 in *Individualism and Economic Order*.

———. *The Constitution of Liberty*. London: Routledge & Kegan Paul; Chicago: Univ. of Chicago Press, 1960.

———. *The Counter-Revolution of Science*. Glencoe, Ill.: Free Press, 1952.

———. *Geldtheorie und Konjunkturtheorie*. Vienna and Leipzig: Hölder-Pichler-Temsky, 1929. Translated by Nicholas Kaldor and H. M. Croome as *Monetary Theory and the Trade Cycle*. London: Jonathan Cape, 1933, and New York: Harcourt, Brace, 1933.

———. *Individualism and Economic Order*. London: Routledge & Kegan Paul; Chicago: Univ. of Chicago Press, 1948.

———. *John Stuart Mill and Harriet Taylor*. London: Routledge & Kegan Paul; Chicago: Univ. of Chicago Press, 1951.

———. *Law, Legislation and Liberty*. 3 vols. London: Routledge & Kegan Paul; Chicago: Univ. of Chicago Press, 1973–79.

———. Letters to Karl Popper. In the archive of the Hoover Institution, Stanford, California, 1952, 1960.

———. *Prices and Production*. London: Routledge, 1931.

————. *The Pure Theory of Capital*. London: Routledge & Kegan Paul; Chicago: Univ. of Chicago Press, 1941.

————. *The Road to Serfdom*. London: Routledge and Sons; Chicago: Univ. of Chicago Press, 1944.

————. *The Sensory Order*. Chicago: Univ. of Chicago Press, 1952.

————. *Studies in Philosophy, Politics, and Economics*. Chicago: Univ. of Chicago Press, 1967. Includes "Degrees of Explanation," "Rules, Perception and Intelligibility," and "The Theory of Complex Phenomena."

————. "Das amerikanische Bankwesen seit der Reform von 1914." *Der Österreichische Volkswirt* (Vienna) 17, nos. 29–32 (April 18 & 25, 1925; May 9 & 16, 1925).

————. "Degrees of Explanation." *British Journal for the Philosophy of Science* (Edinburgh and London) 6, no. 23 (November 1955): 209–25.

————. "Economics and Knowledge." *Economica* (London), n.s. 4, no. 13 (February 1937): 33–54. Essay also published in *Individualism and Economic Order*.

————. "Gibt es einen Widersinn des Sparens?" *Zeitschrift für Nationalökonomie* (Vienna) 1, no. 3 (November 15, 1929): 387–429. Translated by Nicholas Kaldor and Georg Tugendhat as "The Paradox of Saving." *Economica* (London) 11, no. 32 (May 1931): 125–69.

————. "Das intertemporale Gleichgewichtssystem der Preise und die Bewegungen des 'Geldwertes.'" *Weltwirtschaftliches Archiv* (Jena) 28, no. 1 (July 1928): 33–76.

————. "The Sensory Order After 25 Years." In vol. 2 of *Cognition and the Symbolic Processes*, ed. Walter B. Weimer and David S. Palermo, 287–93. Hillsdale, N.J.: Lawrence Erlbaum, 1982.

————. "Die Währungspolitik der Vereinigten Staaten seit der Überwindung der Krise von 1920." *Zeitschrift für Volkswirtschaft und Sozialpolitik*, N.F. 5 (1925), in two parts, sections 1–3, pp. 25–63, and sections 4–6, pp. 254–317. Section 6 is translated and reprinted in *Money, Capital and Fluctuations: Early Essays*, ed. Roy McCloughry. London: Routledge & Kegan Paul, 1984.

Hicks, John. *Value and Capital*. Oxford: Clarendon Press, 1939.

Keynes, John Maynard. *The Economic Consequences of Mr. Churchill* [1925]. Vol. 9 of *The Collected Writings of John Maynard Keynes*. London: Macmillan, 1971.

————. *The Economic Consequences of the Peace* [1919]. Vol. 2 of *The Collected Writings*. 1971.

————. *The General Theory of Employment, Interest, and Money* [1936]. Vol. 7 of *The Collected Writings*. 1973.

————. Letter to Hayek about *The Road to Serfdom* [June 28, 1944]. In vol. 27 of *The Collected Writings*, 385–88. 1980.

————. *A Tract on Monetary Reform* [1923]. Vol. 4 of *The Collected Writings*. 1971.

————. *A Treatise on Money* [1930]. Vol. 5 of *The Collected Writings*. 1971.

Lachmann, Ludwig M. *Capital and Its Structure*. London: Bell, on behalf of the London School of Economics, 1956.

Mach, Ernst. *Analysis of Sensations*.

Menger, Carl. *Grundsätze der Volkswirtschaftslehre*. Vienna: W. Braunmüller, 1871.

Mill, John Stuart. *Autobiography of John Stuart Mill*. New York: Columbia Univ. Press, 1924.

———. *On Liberty*, ed. McCallum. Oxford: Oxford Univ. Press, 1946.

———. *Untersuchungen über die Methode der Sozialwissenschaften und der Politischen Ökonomie insbesondere*. Leipzig: Duncker und Humblot, 1883.

Nef, John U. *Search for Meaning: The Autobiography of a Nonconformist*. Washington, D.C.: Public Affairs Press, 1973.

Pigou, A. C. *Economics in Practice*. London: Macmillan, 1935.

Popper, Karl. *Logik der Forschung, zur Erkenntnistheorie der modernen Naturwissenschaft*. Vienna: J. Springer, published in the autumn of 1934 with the imprint "1935." Translated as *The Logic of Scientific Discovery*. London: Hutchinson, 1959.

Proust, Marcel. *Remembrance of Things Past*. Translated by C. K. Scott Moncrieff. London and New York: Thomas Seltzer, 1924.

———. *Swann's Way*. Modern Library edition, 1934.

Schlick, Moritz. *Allgemeine Erkenntnislehre*. Berlin: J. Springer, 1918.

Schumpeter, Joseph. *Capitalism, Socialism, and Democracy*. New York and London: Harper and Bros., 1942.

Spann, Othmar. *Fundament der Volkswirtschaftslehre*. Jena: G. Fischer, 1918.

Weismann, August. *Vorträge über Deszendenztheorie*. Jena: G. Fischer, 1902.

Woolf, Virginia. "Mr. Bennett and Mrs. Brown." In vol. 1 of *Collected Essays*, ed. Leonard Woolf. London: Chatto & Windus, 1966. Originally a paper read to the Heretics, Cambridge, on May 18, 1924.

INDEX OF PERSONS AND PLACES

Editor's note: Information is given here to clarify the relationship of some of these persons to the development of Hayek's ideas and career.

Achilles, 45

Acton, Lord John (1834–1902; British classical liberal historian and political thinker. Author, *Lectures on Modern History* and *The History of Freedom and Other Essays*. See *The Collected Works of F. A. Hayek*, vol. 4), 14

Adams, Henry (1838–1918), 16

Andromache, 45

Aristotle (384–332 B.C.), 16, 25, 47

Athens, 129

Attlee, Clement, later Earl Attlee (1883–1967; British statesman. Labour Party leader; prime minister, 1945–51; lecturer at London School of Economics, 1912–23, interrupted by wartime service), 106f

Bad Ischl, 60

Balogh, Lord Thomas (1905–1985; Hungarian-born political economist. Advisor to the Bank of England; fellow and lecturer at Balliol College, Oxford; later advisor to Harold Wilson's Labour governments. Attended functions at the London School of Economics;

critic of J. M. Keynes's optimism toward postwar recovery), 87

Barone, Enrico (1859–1924; Italian economist. Pioneer in mathematical economics; supporter of rational socialist planning), 79

Bartley, William W., III (1934–1990), 35

Basle, 60, 136

Bauer, Otto (1881–1938; Viennese social theorist. Student of Eugen von Böhm-Bawerk; leading tactician of Austrian Social Democratic Party, 1920–34; author, *The Austrian Revolution* (1923)), 56

Beales, Hugh Lancelot (1889–1988; British economic historian. Taught at the London School of Economics, 1931–56; author, *The Early English Socialists* (1929) and *The Industrial Revolution* (1932)), 82

Becker, Gary (1930–), 144

Beckhart, Benjamin H. (1897–1975; American economist. Professor at Columbia University, 1921–63; editor, *Banking Systems* (1954) and *The Federal Reserve System* (1972)), 66